Washington and the American Revolution

A Guide to the Campaigns in Pennsylvania & New Jersey

by

Anita D. Blackaby

The Council of American Revolutionary Sites
Washington Crossing, PA

This project was funded by a grant from:
The William Penn Foundation

Additional funding was received from:
Bergen County Historical Society
Office of New Jersey Heritage,
Department of Environmental Protection
The Friends of Valley Forge
Forbes Foundation
Patriotic Order Sons of America
Pennsylvania Historical & Museum Commission
Princeton Battlefield Area Preservation Society
Rockingham Association
Ms. Marilyn L. Steinbright
Techtron Graphic Arts
Washington Crossing Foundation

Design:
Anita D. Blackaby & James R. Blackaby

Illustrations:
The historic site illustrations were drawn by Caroline Webb, Old Barracks Museum, with the exception of the Johnson Ferry House, drawn by John Tracy, Philadelphia, PA. The historic engravings are taken from John Grafton, *The American Revolution: A Picture Source Book*, Dover Publications, except were indicated.

Cover Illustration:
Edward Hicks, Washington Crossing The Delaware River. Bridge sign painted on a wooden panel, c. 1834. From the collection of the Mercer Museum of The Bucks County Historical Society, Doylestown, PA.

Printing:
American Brochure
Ivyland, PA

This book was made possible by the cooperative efforts of the COUNCIL of AMERICAN REVOLUTIONARY SITES (CARS). The council is a consortium of historic organizations in the greater Delaware Valley, dedicated to the promotion of the many Revolutionary Sites in the area. Address all inquiries to:

COUNCIL of AMERICAN REVOLUTIONARY SITES
Washington Crossing Historic Park
Washington Crossing, PA 18977

Library of Congress Catalog Card Number: 86-070173
ISBN: 0-9616323-0-5

ABOUT THE AUTHOR

Anita D. Blackaby is a native of Detroit, Michigan where she grew up. She attended the University of Michigan and Wayne State University. Her university training was in education, and she taught for several years before becoming Curator of Education for the Detroit Historical Museum, a position she held for five years.

In 1984 she moved to Doylestown, Pennsylvania and became a consultant for museum programs. She has worked for the Council of American Revolutionary Sites, Atwater Kent Museum, and the Brandywine Battlefield. Her work for the Council of American Revolutionary Sites includes this publication and a brochure, *American Revolutionary Times.*.

CONTENTS

CONTENTS — ACTIVITIES

FOREWORD

Philadelphia was the largest city in America at the beginning of the Revolution. It was a commercial and cultural center as well. For this reason the city attracted people and events, and it became the legislative and political center for the new nation. Two major military campaigns were fought in its environs. It fell to the British and then to the Americans in turn. Our nation was forged here.

Many of the historic sites where these events occurred can be seen and visited today. At these historic sites one can get a glimpse of the issues and the people who fought in the Revolution and who made the history which formed our country.

In fact, visiting these places is a very popular experience. About 40 percent (10,000,000 people) of the regional population visits these sites every year. These visitors come to view a place where something intimately connected with their past took place. Even so, it is difficult for visitors who visit only one or two sites at a time, to relate the historic site they are seeing with other sites or with the whole Revolutionary War.

At a meeting of the Council of American Revolutionary Sites (CARS), we discussed the need to show school children and other visitors how each Revolutionary War site fitted into the whole history of the Revolution and with other sites. Out of that meeting came two publications. The first, ***American Revolutionary Times*** *is primarily an educational brochure aimed at the general public. The other is this book which we hope will help make trips to the Revolutionary War sites more meaningful.*

This book is intended to help visitors to recognize that the Revolutionary War happened all around them, that the events and historic sites have a relation to each other and are part of a continuum connecting the past with the present. The guide is intended primarily for use by teachers, but it also addresses the needs of families and the general public. Each site visited should be seen as just one stage, of many stages, upon which the Revolution was played out. We have selected all the important sites involved in the Revolutionary War in the Philadelphia area. There are 25 of them. We selected for inclusion in this book those which are maintained as historic properties or museums and which are open to the public on a regular basis. You can visit them in a logical sequence. If you start out with the 1776 retreat of the American Army at Fort Lee and follow it from historic site to historic site through the Battle of Monmouth in the summer of 1778, you will have seen almost every place related to the War in this area and know something about the events and the people who made them. You will see a lot of fine historic sites and meet a number of interesting people.

Daniel B Reibel
for the Council of American Revolutionary Sites

INTRODUCTION

From 1776 to 1779 the greater Delaware Valley area of Pennsylvania and New Jersey served as the stage for the American Revolution. All of the key players were positioned in the area — Congress in Philadelphia, British headquarters in New York City, and General George Washington in the field directing operations. As the Revolution unfolded, many significant events that determined the final outcome of the Revolution occurred in the area. Today these events are remembered and commemorated by the numerous historic sites dedicated to the American Revolution.

Residents and visitors of the greater Delaware Valley area are most fortunate in having front row seats to the events of 1776 to 1779. Nearly every significant military and civil action is represented by a historic site. Today we can go and visit the scene of Washington's winter encampment at Valley Forge, the building in which the anxious Congress met in Philadelphia, the house where the Battle of Germantown was planned, the field on which General Hugh Mercer was mortally wounded during the Battle of Princeton, or the river banks where Washington decided to make the historic crossing that Christmas night in 1776 that led to victory in Trenton. We are surrounded by history. The roads we travel daily follow the routes that our nation's founders trod. Many of the houses that we pass daily are houses that were standing at the time of the Revolution. We may have built houses or shopping centers in fields that witnessed dramatic events of our country's birth, but for those who take the time to look, the story of our nation's founding can be seen all around us preserved in our historic sites.

In some instances, the federal or state government has preserved places where our history unfolded. In other instances, local groups of interested individuals have formed in order to save a significant site. Some of the sites are very large and well staffed. Some of them are small with only a staff of one. Regardless of size, each preserves an equally important aspect of our nation's birth. Each offers a unique opportunity to learn about and experience the past.

The teaching methods that are employed at the various sites include slide shows, films, guided tours, galleries of artifacts, restored homes, books and pamphlets, historic reenactments, first person interpretations, special events, and hands-on activities. All of the sites seek to communicate the great significance of the actions that happened in the greater Delaware Valley during those crucial years.

This book was conceived as a guide to the Revolutionary sites of the Delaware Valley and their interpretive programs. It provides an outline to those historic events, a description of the sites, and a comment on their educational offerings. The activity pages and historic documents in the guide are designed to help young people learn about the past in both a fun and exciting manner. A special thanks to the many institutions and individuals for their help in the preparation of this guide. The executive committee of the Council of American Revolutionary Sites has provided considerable direction in the preparation of this book.

The committee includes: Ann Hawkes Hutton, Chairman of the Board, Washington Crossing Foundation; Paul Taylor, Chief Curator, Office of New Jersey Heritage; John Tyler, Chief of Interpretation, Valley Forge National Historical Park; Daniel B Reibel, Chief, Eastern Regional Division, Pennsylvania Historical & Museum Commission; Walter Robson, Curator, Washington Crossing Foundation; as well as Marilyn C. Solvay, former Historic Site Administrator, Brandywine Battlefield Park. Staff members from the twenty five sites provided essential information and material for the book. They include: Robert B. Britton, Assistant Curator/Interpreter, Washington Crossing State Park, NJ; Mary E. Brod, former Site Administrator, Pottsgrove Mansion; Anne L. B. Burnett, Museum Educator, Washington Crossing Historic Park; John Dwyer, Chief of Interpretation, Morristown National Historical Park; Richard W. Eberle, Park Superintendent, Fort Washington State Park; Jennifer Esler, Executive Director, Cliveden; Mary Eileen Fouratt, Education Coordinator, Monmouth County Historical Association;

David C. Forney, Assistant Chief of Interpretation, Valley Forge National Historical Park; Albert T. Gamon, Director/Administrator, Peter Wentz Farmstead; Jeanette Graff, Interpreter, Rockingham; Suzanne Keenan, Curator, Valley Forge Historical Society; William A. Kingsley, Director, Betsy Ross House; Cynthia Koch, Director, Old Barracks Museum; Alan P. Koch, Landscape Architect, Red Bank Battlefield; Thomas A. Lainhoff, Historic Site Administrator, Washington Crossing Historic Park, PA; Stephen McGinnis, Curator, Dey Mansion; Pat Millen, former Interpreter, Clarke House, Princeton Battlefield State Park; John Mills, Curator, Clarke House, Princeton Battlefield State Park; James Mosetter, President, Olde Fort Mifflin Historical Society, Inc.; John Muller, Director, Fort Lee Historic Park; T. Mark Pitchell, Superintendent, Monmouth Battlefield State Park; Brenda Reigle, Historic Site Administrator, Hope Lodge; Russell P. Smith, Chief, Interpretive Branch of Support Services, Independence National Historical Park; Harry Kels Swan, Curator, Washington Crossing State Park, NJ; Susan L. Taylor, former Curator, Wallace House & Old Dutch Parsonage; Anne S. Woodward, Historic Site Administrator, Brandywine Battlefield Park; Keven Wright, Curator, Steuben House.

British soldiers with artillery

September 5 - October 26, 1774

Continental Congress Formed Delegates Meet in Philadelphia

As tension with Great Britain increased, the Colonies realized the need to band together to attempt to resolve their common problem. No central system of government existed in the Colonies although each Colony had a tradition of government at the local level. A meeting of delegates from each of the Colonies was scheduled for Philadelphia. All of the Colonies except Georgia sent delegates to the First Continental Congress which met in Carpenter's Hall on September 5, 1774. Through a series of resolutions, the Congress denounced the oppresive rule of the British, but more importantly, they laid the foundation for our present system of government. It was apparent that the conflicts with Britain would not be easily resolved, so a second Continental Congress was scheduled for May, 1775.

In April fighting broke out between British redcoats and local militiamen at Lexington and Concord in Massachusetts. The British retreated to Boston, while an army of citizen-soldiers quickly laid siege to the city. It was this army that the Congress was called upon to adopt in June of 1775 at the Second Continental Congress.

Meeting in the Pennsylvania State House (Independence Hall) in Philadelphia, the Second Congress debated the momentous question of establishing an army for the Colonies. By the middle of June they resolved to adopt the motley army surrounding Boston, issued a call for troops from other Colonies, and appointed George Washington Commander-in-Chief of the American troops.

INDEPENDENCE NATIONAL HISTORICAL PARK
Philadelphia, Pennsylvania

For the next eight years the Congress struggled with the burden of maintaining forces in the field to match the awesome might of the British regulars. Efforts to recruit soldiers, raise money, and furnish supplies were all hampered by the Congress' lack of authority over the Colonies. At the same time, the delegates jealously guarded civilian control of the government against possible encroachment by the military. With these forces at work, final victory against Britain was anything but certain.

The seat of the new government, Philadelphia, became an important prize of war. Not only was it the capital, it was also the largest city and an important seaport. During the war for independence, many battles would be fought and many lives lost to defend this city which Robert Morris called the "heart" of the new nation, Philadelphia.

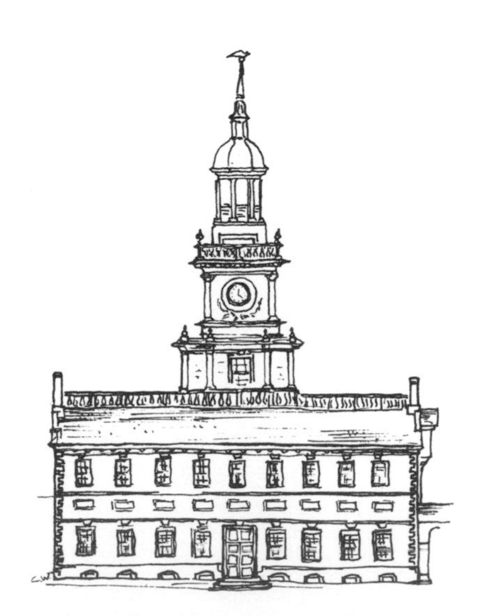

Independence National Historical Park

313 Walnut Street • Philadelphia, Pennsylvania 19106 • 215-597-8974

Independence National Historical Park was established by Congress as a tangible reminder of the founding and early growth of the United States of America. The park contains about forty buildings located on forty-two acres of land in downtown Philadelphia. Many of the buildings within the park have direct and fundamental connections with the struggle for independence.

Independence Hall — From the Assembly Room of Independence Hall, the Second Continental Congress exerted control over the military affairs of the emerging United States, worked to establish a political confederation, and directed the effort to secure foreign recognition and support. American prisoners were housed in the Long Room on the 2nd floor during the British occupation of Philadelphia.

Graff House — This reconstruction of the house where Thomas Jefferson lived while writing the Declaration of Independence is dedicated to interpreting the story of the man and the document.

Army/Navy Museum — Located in the reconstructed home of Quaker merchant Joseph Pemberton, this museum provides an overview of the Army and Navy during the Revolution.

Marine Corps Memorial Museum — The exhibits in this reconstruction of the Carpenters' Company's New Hall focus on the contributions of the United States Marines to victory in the Revolution.

Carpenters' Hall — Still owned and operated by the Carpenters' Company of Philadelphia, Carpenters' Hall served as the meeting place for the First Continental Congress and was used in the Revolution as a hospital and an arsenal.

The City Tavern — The original City Tavern served briefly as Washington's headquarters before the Battle of Brandywine and was the scene of the funeral of General Hugh Mercer who was killed at the Battle of Princeton.

RESOURCES
Numerous restored & furnished historic buildings; special events.

VISITOR CENTER
Film; bookstore; interpretive exhibits.

EDUCATIONAL PROGRAMS
Independence Hall Children's Program is available for students in grades K-3. Reservations for this free one-hour program are required. Offered fall and spring only. Call 215-597-8974.

The Philadelphia Public Schools offer special on-site educational programs for their students. Contact the Museum Education Program at 215-299-7778 for information and reservations.

EDUCATIONAL MATERIALS
A pre-visit slide kit and the film "Independence" are available free for loan. Guidebooks and publications are available through: Eastern National Park and Monument Association, 313 Walnut Street, Philadelphia, PA 19106, 215-597-2569.

TOUR INFORMATION
Tours begin at the Visitor Center with the 28-minute film "Independence" (call for schedule). Maps and program information are available here. Admission to Independence Hall is by tour only and is on a first-come, first-served basis. Guided tours of other areas of the park are not available, but rangers are stationed in the buildings to interpret them. Reservations are not accepted, but a park folder and teacher's guide is available for teachers planning a visit.

SUGGESTED ITINERARY
Half-day Tour: Visitor Center; Carpenters' Hall (exterior only); Independence Hall; Liberty Bell Pavilion; Franklin Court.

Full-day Tour: Visitor Center; Carpenters' Hall; Independence Hall; Congress Hall; Old City Hall; Graff House; Liberty Bell Pavilion; Franklin Court; Second Bank of the United States.

FOOD SERVICE
A variety of food service is available in the area. Picnicking is allowed throughout the park. No indoor facilities are available.

ADMISSION
Free

HOURS
Daily, 9:00 a.m. to 5:00 p.m. Extended summer hours.

LOCATION & PARKING
Visitor Center -Third & Chestnut Streets. Vehicle & bus parking 125 Second Street between Chestnut & Walnut Streets.

June 15, 1775

Congress Authorizes National Army Washington Commander-In-Chief

With full-fledged war more likely every day, the Americans needed to defend themselves against the British. The task of putting together an army was not an easy one for the Continental Congress. In the past, communities throughout the Colonies had defended themselves with local militia units. Each militia unit was independent from every other one and no uniformity in military practice, equipment or dress existed. These units were not adequate to defend the Colonies from the well-trained and organized British army. Congress, in an effort to form a strong organized fighting force, agreed to raise ten companies of riflemen from Pennsylvania, Maryland, and Virginia to join the militia defending Boston. Under the command of George Washington these men formed the core of the Continental army.

With Washington at its head, the Continental army was subdivided into functional organizational units. Groups of individual soldiers were formed into companies, ideally consisting of eighty men. Companies were commanded by captains with the aid of lieutenants. Typically, eight companies from adjacent geographic areas were combined to form a regiment or battalion under the command of a colonel. Regiments were organized into larger units called brigades and commanded by a brigadier or brigadier general. The brigadiers reported directly to Washington. This volunteer army of farmers, artisans, merchants, doctors, and lawyers, ranging in age from 14 to 65, united to fight for the newly formed nation.

Tom Paine Explains the Importance of the Revolution

The sun never shined on a cause of greater worth. 'Tis not the affair of a city, a county, a province, or a kingdom, but of a continent — of at least one eighth part of the habitable globe. 'Tis not the concern of a day, a year, or an age; posterity are virtually involved in the contest, and will be more or less affected, even to the end of time, by the proceedings now.

From *Common Sense* by Thomas Paine

June 17, 1775, *Charlestown, MA*
Patriots attack British at Bunker Hill, hope of conciliation lost.

August 23, 1775, *England*
King George III declares the Colonies in rebellion.

January 10, 1776, *Philadelphia, PA*
Thomas Paine urges the Colonies to declare independence in *Common Sense*.

July 4, 1776

Congress Unanimously Approves Declaration of Independence

By June of 1776 the Colonies had been at war with Britain for over a year. However, there was still debate over whether the intent of the Colonies should be independence or peaceful reconciliation with the mother country. It was up to the Second Continental Congress, meeting in the Pennsylvania State House (Independence Hall) in Philadelphia, to resolve the issue.

Not all of the delegates or the citizens of the Colonies agreed that the time was right to dissolve political ties with Great Britain. On June 7, 1776 the issue was brought to a head when Richard Henry Lee of Virginia introduced a resolution calling for independence. Congress did not immediately decide this matter, putting off debate by establishing a committee "...to prepare a declaration to the effect of the said resolution."

Congress appointed John Adams, Thomas Jefferson, Benjamin Franklin, Robert Livingston, and Roger Sherman to draft a Declaration of Independence. Thomas Jefferson was the principal author. For almost a month Jefferson labored to find the right words to express to the world why the Colonies had taken up arms against Britain. On July 2nd Congress approved Lee's resolution for independence and began to review Jefferson's draft of the Declaration of Independence. For two days Congress debated words and phrases and made changes so that the document would be acceptable to all. On July 4, 1776 the Declaration of Independence was officially adopted by Congress. A new nation was born.

Independence Declared

We hold these truths to be self-evident, that all men are created equal, that they are endowed by their Creator with certain unalienable Rights, that among these are Life, Liberty and the Pursuit of Happiness. That to secure these rights, Governments are instituted among Men, deriving their just powers from the consent of the governed. That whenever any Form of Government becomes destructive of these ends, it is the Right of the People to alter or to abolish it, and to institute new Government,...

From the Declaration of Independence.

The Declaration of Independence

Although the Declaration of Independence is now recognized as an expression of human rights, its original purpose was to explain the reasons for fighting the British. Thomas Jefferson, the principal author of the Declaration, said the Declaration was written "...to place before mankind the common sense of the subject, in terms so plain and firm as to command their assent...."

These are some of the complaints the Declaration makes:

> ***For quartering large bodies of armed troops among us:***
>
> ***For protecting them, by a mock Trial, from Punishment for any Murders which they should commit on the Inhabitants of these States:***
>
> ***For cutting off our Trade with all parts of the world:***
>
> ***For imposing taxes on us without our Consent:***
>
> ***For depriving us in many cases, of the benefits of Trial by Jury:***
>
> ***For transporting us beyond Seas to be tried for pretended offenses:***

Instructions

These are just a few of the many injustices by the British against the Colonies that were mentioned in the Declaration of Independence. King George responded to the Declaration of Independence by continuing the War against the Colonies. The King did not have to take this course of action. He could have responded to the Declaration of Independence by recognizing the grievances and trying to solve the problems or by granting independence to the Colonies.

As King George III, how would you have responded to the injustices in the Declaration of Independence. On the following page write your response to the Colonies.

George III Proclaims ______________________________

______________________, *1776*

____

____

____

____

____

____

____

____

____

____

____

____

____

____

____

____

____

Given at our Court at St. James's the ______________________ *day of*

______________________, *one thousand seven hundred and seventy-six,*

in the sixteenth year of our reign.

GOD save the KING

July, 1776

Americans Hold New York City: British Prepare to Attack

After the successful siege of Boston, Washington turned his attention to the defense of New York and the Hudson Valley. Along with the construction of fortifications at New York City and Long Island, he built Fort Washington and Fort Lee just north of New York City along the Hudson River.

The British planned to control the length of the Hudson with the overwhelming dominance of the Royal Navy. If successful, they would split the Colonies in half and bring an early end to the Revolution.

King George III, wanting to end the Revolution as quickly as possible, sent the largest armada of ships and troops that had ever left England's shores to New York City. By mid-August General Sir William Howe, British Commander-in-Chief, assembled an army of over 31,000 British, Hessian and loyalist troops on Staten Island. Washington's army was spread throughout the area in a feeble attempt to defend the city. Howe's unified, professional troops moved against the Americans and emerged victorious at the Battle of Long Island. Washington's brilliant strategic retreat across the East River after the battle saved the American forces. The army continued to lose ground at the Battles of Harlem Heights and White Plains. Washington faced the task of maintaining his dwindling army. In the face of defeat, thousands of patriots abandoned the cause. Morale remained low among the remaining troops because of defeat, troop desertion, supply shortages, fatigue, and lack of confidence. Washington, realizing he could no longer defend the city, retreated to Fort Washington and Fort Lee which served as the Hudson River defenses.

The Conditions at Fort Lee

Our situation there was exceedingly cramped, the place being on a narrow neck of land between the North [Hudson] River and the Hackensack. Our force was inconsiderable, being not one-fourth so great as Howe could bring against us. We had no army at hand to have relieved the garrison had we shut ourselves up and stood on the defense.

From *The Crisis* by Thomas Paine

THE RETREAT FROM BROOKLYN HEIGHTS
August 29-30, 1776

August 27, 1776, *Long Island, NY*
Americans defeated by British at Battle of Long Island

September 6-7, 1776, *New York Harbor*
Patriots attempt first submarine attack in "American Turtle."

November 16, 1776, *Fort Washington, NY*
British attack and take Fort Washington, 3,000 captured.

November 20, 1776

Fort Lee Evacuated: British Secure in New York

Control of the Hudson River was of strategic importance to the Americans and the British. Whoever held the river controlled access to and from the New England Colonies, allowing the movement of troops and supplies. In an attempt to hold the Hudson River against the British, Washington constructed two fortifications across from each other on the river north of New York City. In July of 1776 work was begun on Fort Lee, named for General Charles Lee who visited the area after his successful defense of Charleston, North Carolina. On the opposite shore work had already begun on Fort Washington.

On July 12, Admiral Richard Howe, brother of General William Howe, sent two British naval vessels up the Hudson River. Cannon fire from Fort Washington had little effect on their passage. Washington then ordered that work on Fort Lee continue as quickly as possible. At Major General Israel Putnam's suggestion, sunken ships were placed in the river channel to block the river. With these obstructions and artillery fire from the sister forts it was felt that no British ships could sail up the Hudson without sustaining severe losses.

From August to October the British and American forces battled for control of New York City, with disastrous results for the Americans. On November 16th Fort Washington fell to an overwhelming assault by the British force. Washington, realizing that with the loss of Fort Washington Fort Lee was of little military value, made preparations to evacuate his remaining army through New Jersey.

FORT LEE HISTORIC PARK

Fort Lee, New Jersey

On November 20th General Cornwallis ferried over 6,000 British and Hessian troops across the Hudson River north of Fort Lee. After climbing the steep Palisades, the cliffs along the west bank of the river, they moved to take the Fort. When word of the crossing reached Washington he ordered an immediate retreat before his army was cut off and captured by the British. Defending the unfinished Fort while greatly outnumbered was not a practical option for Washington. Caught by surprise, the Americans had to leave behind most of their supplies and heavy artillery in an effort to safely evacuate the troops and avoid capture. These were indeed the darkest days

for the Revolution and led to Thomas Paine's famous words: "These are the times that try men's souls." Washington would later order these words read to the troops before the crossing of the Delaware prior to the Battle of Trenton.

Fort Lee Historic Park

Hudson Terrace • Fort Lee, New Jersey 07024 • 201-461-3956

Fort Lee Historic Park occupies approximately 33 acres on the Palisades, encompassing the area where the gun batteries and magazine of Fort Lee were located during the Revolutionary War. The reconstruction of this historic site has been conceived by the Palisades Interstate Park Commission to provide both an educational and a scenic experience.

The park area contains walkways and scenic overlooks commanding panoramic views of the Hudson River and the Manhattan skyline, as well as replicas of the Continental Army's 1776 fortifications. From the original maps and sketches the architects designed historically accurate reconstructions of the three gun batteries and the firing step of the Revolutionary War period. The original gun emplacements were made of fascines (bundles of saplings tightly tied together and stacked in two layers with earth in between). Because this perishable material was not suitable for long-term use in the park, the restored fortifications are constructed of synthetic materials. The surfaces of the embrasures — the spaces in the battery through which the guns were fired — are plastered over, as they were originally, to keep the fascines from igniting when the guns fired.

The firing step protected foot soldiers who defended the approach to the fort from the west. It is equipped with fraises — sharply pointed stakes mounted at an angle to repel attackers. Its restored form uses the materials of the original — stone bases topped by hand-hewn logs.

An authentic 18th century soldiers' hut with a well, wood-shed, and bake oven serves as the focal point for many interpretive programs.

RESOURCES
Reconstructed Revolutionary Fort: gun batteries; firing step soldiers' hut with well, wood shed, and bake oven; special events. 18th century activities are demonstrated at the soldiers' hut during summer months and on weekends throughout the year. Call for information.

VISITOR CENTER & MUSEUM
Two floors of audio-visual displays, detailed exhibits, and a short film present the story of the evacuation of the fort and the retreat through New Jersey led by George Washington.

EDUCATIONAL PROGRAMS
School children studying the Revolution or early American history can visit Fort Lee and experience life as recruits in an 18th century army. This 18th Century 4-hour "Living History" program combines discussion, demonstration, and participation to give students a complete lesson in colonial military life. A fee is charged and reservations are required. Call for information.

TOUR INFORMATION
The excellent exhibits and introductory film presented in the visitor center will provide a firm background for a tour of the reconstructed fort and soldiers' hut. Numerous outdoor signs aid in interpreting the historic park. Guided tours are available by reservation during the summer only. All groups are required to make advance reservations.

FOOD SERVICE
Picnic area available. Barbecues & open fires not permitted.

ADMISSION
Free

HOURS
Spring & Summer: Daily, 10:00 a.m. to 5:00 p.m. Fall & Winter: Wednesday—Sunday, 10:00 a.m. to 5:00 p.m. Closed January & February. Call for information.

LOCATION & PARKING
On Hudson Terrace in Fort Lee, NJ, south of George Washington Bridge. From routes 4, 46, 80, & 95 take Fort Lee/Palisades Interstate Parkway exit. Vehicle and bus parking on park grounds. Parking fee from April through November: $10.00/bus; $2.00/automobile.

November 21, 1776, *Passaic, NJ*
Washington retreats from Hackensack, troops cross Passaic river.

November 23, 1776, *Newark, NJ*
With British in pursuit Washington continues retreat and reaches Newark.

December 1, 1776, *Brunswick, NJ*
Washington orders all water craft along Delaware River secured.

November 20, 1776

Americans Retreat from Ft. Lee: 2,000 Cross Hackensack River

Life in the bustling little hamlet of New Bridge was changed dramatically in the fall of 1776 as the American Revolution raged on around it. New Bridge was the site of a house and gristmill owned by Jan Zabriskie along the banks of the Hackensack River. Today it is known as the Steuben House. The building of the "New Bridge" across the river in 1744 brought commercial traffic to the area as it was the first river crossing above Newark Bay. Flour ground at the gristmill was shipped weekly to New York City on Zabriskie's sloop, which returned with merchandise to trade in his store. Iron from the Ramapo Mountains was carted to the New Bridge landing for shipment to market. As a result of this business activity, in 1752 Jan Zabriskie doubled the size of the house to twelve rooms heated by seven fireplaces.

On November 20, 1776 more than six thousand British and Hessian troops crossed the Hudson River to attack Fort Lee. Washington rode out from his headquarters in Hackensack and led the fleeing American garrison of the fort over the New Bridge. A large part of the American army was saved from entrapment on the peninsula between the Hudson and Hackensack Rivers. The old wooden span that carried them to safety was later dubbed "The Bridge That Saved A Nation."

Throughout the War New Bridge stood in disputed territory, located between British-occupied New York and Colonial-occupied Philadelphia. This strategic point changed hands all through the war, serving as battle-ground, encampment site, headquarters, and fort to defend the bridge.

STEUBEN HOUSE

River Edge, New Jersey

Shortly before the outbreak of the Revolution, the Steuben House was owned by Jan Zabriskie, Junior, who inherited the homestead upon his father's death. Zabriskie was accused of passing military intelligence to the British and was arrested by American raiders in 1777. He fled to British-held Manhattan. In January of 1781 it was determined that Jan Zabriskie had joined the Army of the King of Great Britain, and the State of New Jersey confiscated his estate.

The New Jersey State Legislature presented the Zabriskie estate to Major General Baron von Steuben

on December 23, 1783 in gratitude for his services to the Continental army. The Baron was a Prussian officer who helped to train and organize the Continental army at Valley Forge. Von Steuben never took possession of the property, and it was eventually sold back to the Zabriskie family.

Steuben House

1209 Main Street • River Edge, New Jersey 07661 • 201-487-1739

Near the heart of Bergen County, at the Hackensack River, stands a landmark of early sandstone architecture associated with the Prussian Inspector-General of the Continental troops, Baron von Steuben. The house is located on a 420 acre plot purchased in 1682 by Cornelius Matheus. In 1695 his son Matheus Corneliusson, deeded the property to David Ackerman of Hackensack who erected the first gristmill on the estate. His son, Johannes, a shoemaker, inherited that portion of his father's estate bordering the River, and the oldest portion of the Steuben House probably dates from the time of Johannes' marriage in 1713. His son, Niclas, sold the house and mill in 1745 to Jan Zabriskie of Hackensack.

During the Sesquicentennial of the United States in 1926, the State Legislature appropriated money to purchase the Steuben House as a shrine of historic significance. The State of New Jersey acquired the house and one surrounding acre in 1928. Since its restoration in 1939, the Steuben House has displayed the museum collection of the Bergen County Historical Society. It is owned and staffed by the Division of Parks and Forestry, New Jersey Department of Environmental Protection.

The Steuben House contains many objects of historic interest acquired by the Bergen County Historical Society since it was established in 1902. The artifacts on display are primarily of local manufacture and use. Outstanding examples of 18th century furnishings, local pottery, antique dolls, and toys are on exhibit. The textile collection contains antique apparel, local quilts, and woven spreads. An Indian dug-out canoe, unearthed in Hackensack in 1868, is on view in the garret gallery. Other items on display include fine examples of antique ceramics, metalwork, paintings, and folk art, as well as accessories of everyday life in earlier times.

RESOURCES
Restored & furnished 18th century house; exhibits; special events; additional historic buildings on property.

EDUCATIONAL PROGRAMS
An outreach program, coordinated by the Junior League and the Steuben House, is available to local 4th and 5th grade classes. Docents travel to area schools to present a program on the history and geography of the Steuben House and the surrounding area. Call for information.

TOUR INFORMATION
A staff member escorts groups or individuals through the Steuben House on a 30 to 60 minute tour. Tours are limited to 25 per group. Advance reservations required for group tours. Self-guided tours of the house are not available. Call for reservations.

FOOD SERVICE
Picnicking is allowed on the grounds, but no shelter or tables are available.

ADMISSION
Suggested donation

HOURS
Wednesday—Saturday, 10:00 a.m. to 12 noon & 1:00 p.m. to 5:00 p.m. Sunday, 2:00 p.m. to 5:00 p.m.

LOCATION & PARKING
1209 Main Street, River Edge, NJ. Call for specific directions. Vehicle and bus parking on park grounds.

Baron von Steuben

December 2, 1776, *Princeton, NJ*
Washington continues to elude British, reaches Princeton.

December 7-8, 1776, *Trenton, NJ*
Americans cross Delaware River. Hold all boats on the Pennsylvania side.

December 8, 1776, *Trenton, NJ*
First British Troops enter Trenton. The lack of boats prevents them from pursuing Americans.

November 21, 1776

Washington & Army on the Run British in Pursuit

After the fall of New York, with the loss of Fort Washington and Fort Lee on the Hudson River, Washington was forced to find a safe haven for his remaining army. British General Charles Cornwallis, Commander of the British force in New Jersey, was in pursuit of Washington and his army. From Newark to Brunswick, Brunswick to Princeton, Princeton to Trenton, the poorly supplied and ill fed army marched as quickly as possible toward the safety of Pennsylvania.

The British pursued the Americans with caution, sending out scouting parties to survey the terrain and to be certain the Americans had not laid a trap for them. To delay the British force, the American rear guard burned bridges and blocked roads. The British were also slowed by the movement of their heavily laden supply wagons and cumbersome cannon. The American army traveled the 100 miles to Trenton in seventeen days, arriving two days ahead of the slower British force.

Washington ordered all boats along a seventy-five mile stretch of the Delaware River to be confiscated and brought to the ferry landing at Trenton. Among them were the huge Durham boats. These forty to sixty foot open boats were used to transport heavy iron ore and pig iron from the Durham Iron Works in Riegelsville, Pennsylvania to market in Philadelphia. These boats transported the army across the Delaware River into Pennsylvania. All other craft were secured on the Pennsylvania side of the river to prevent them from falling into British hands. For the moment the army was safe.

George Washington's Request To Secure Boats On The Delaware

[New] Brunswick, December 1: 1776

Sir

You are to proceed to The Two ferry's near Trentown and to see all the boats there put in the best order with a Sufficiency of Oars and poles and at the same time to Collect all the Additional Boats you [can] from both above and below and have them brought to those ferry's and Secured for the purpose of Carrying over the Troops and Baggage in most expeditious Manner: & for this purpose you will get every Assistance in the power of Quarter Master General & any person in his department. You will particularly attend to the Durham Boats which are very proper for this purpose. The Baggage & Stores of the Army should be got over the River as soon as possible and placed at some Convenient place a little back from it.

I am Sir, Your Most Obt. Servt.

Go: Washington.

The Swan Collection of the American Revolution, Washington Crossing State Park, New Jersey.

" '76" published in Harper's Weekly, July 15, 1876.

Washington's Retreat Across New Jersey — 1776

Washington and his army barely avoided being captured by the British troops as they retreated through New Jersey. By destroying bridges, confiscating boats, blocking roads and attacking the advancing British troops Washington and his men were able to stay ahead of the British. Listed below are some of the significant dates marking Washington's and Howe's movements through New Jersey.

GENERAL WASHINGTON & THE CONTINENTAL ARMY

November 12th
Crossed Hudson River at Stony Point North of Haverstraw.

November 14th
Arrived at Fort Lee, NJ.

November 20th
Evacuated Fort Lee, NJ. Crossed Hackensack River at Hackensack (New Bridge), NJ.

November 21st
Crossed the Passaic River at Passaic, NJ.

November 23rd
Arrived at Newark, NJ.

November 28th
Left Newark, NJ. Traveled through Elizabeth, NJ.

November 29th
Crossed Raritan River. Arrived at New Brunswick, NJ.

December 1st
Left New Brunswick, NJ. Traveled through Princeton to Trenton.

December 3rd
Arrived at Trenton, NJ.

December 7th & 8th
Crossed the Delaware River into Pennsylvania from Trenton, NJ.

December 9th
Established defenses along the Pennsylvania side of the Delaware River.

SIR WILLIAM HOWE & THE BRITISH ARMY

November 16th
Captured Fort Washington.

November 19th
Crossed Hudson River at Yonkers, NY & marched to Closter, NJ.

November 21st
Arrived Fort Lee, NJ

November 22nd
Crossed Hackensack River. Arrived at the Passaic River. Delayed several days in crossing—bridge destroyed and boats gone.

November 28th
Arrived at Newark, NJ

December 1st
Arrived at New Brunswick as American troops depart.

December 8th
Arrived at Trenton as last Americans crossed the Delaware River.

December 9th
Decided they could not cross the Delaware River for lack of boats. Established posts at Bordentown, New Brunswick, Pennington, & Trenton.

Instructions

On the accompanying map of New Jersey mark the routes used by the American and British army to cross the area. Use a blue pencil or marker for the American route and a red pencil or marker for the British route. Include the dates the armies were in each location.

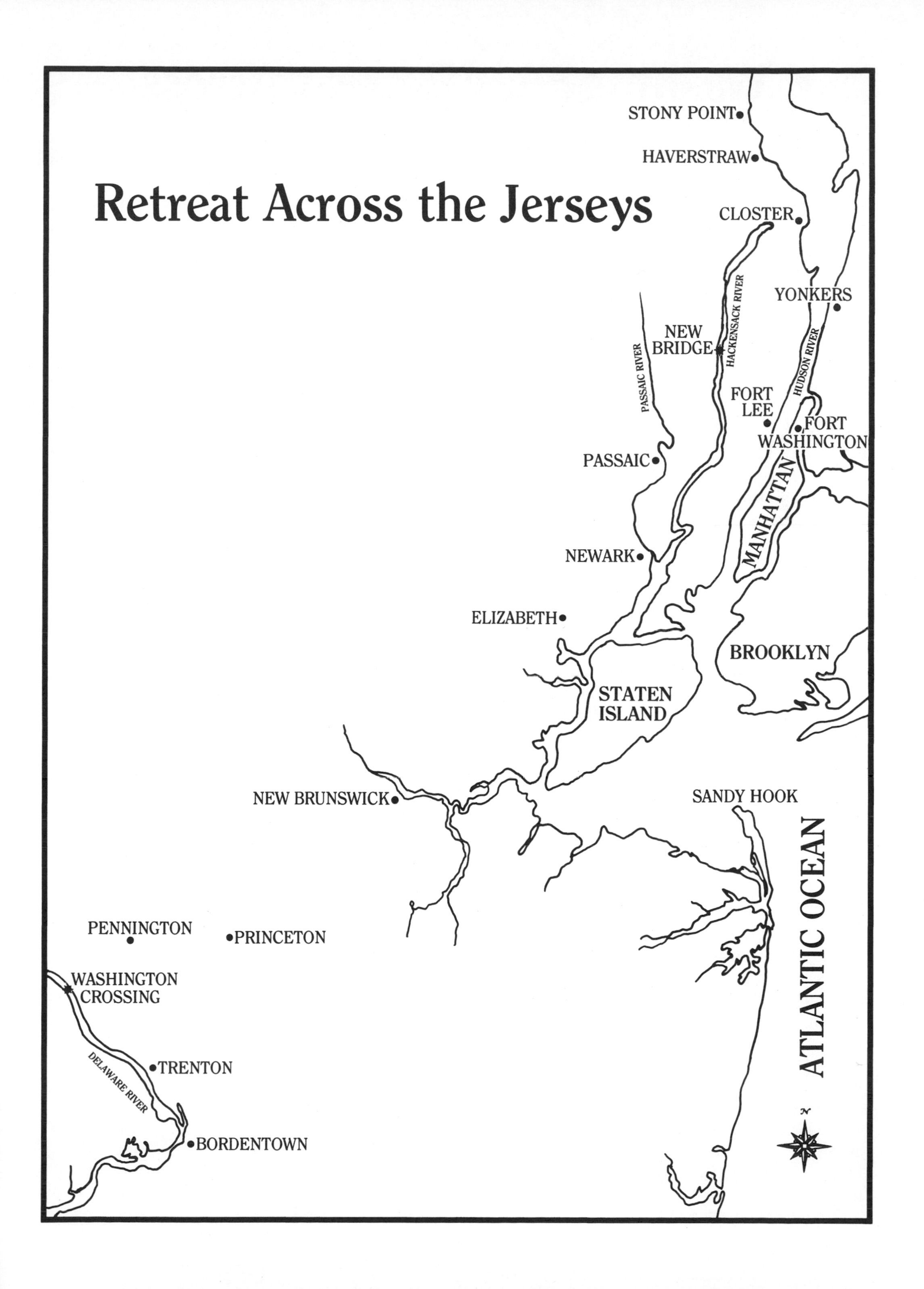

Retreat Across the Jerseys
STONY POINT
HAVERSTRAW
CLOSTER
YONKERS
HACKENSACK RIVER
NEW BRIDGE
PASSAIC RIVER
HUDSON RIVER
FORT LEE
FORT WASHINGTON
PASSAIC
MANHATTAN
NEWARK
ELIZABETH
BROOKLYN
STATEN ISLAND
NEW BRUNSWICK
SANDY HOOK
ATLANTIC OCEAN
PENNINGTON
PRINCETON
WASHINGTON CROSSING
DELAWARE RIVER
TRENTON
BORDENTOWN
N

December 12, 1776, *Philadelphia, PA*
With the British force in New Jersey, Congress resolves to move to Baltimore.

December 13, 1776, *Princeton, NJ*
British announce the campaign suspended until spring.

December 13, 1776, *Basking Ridge, NJ*
General Lee fails to follow Washington's orders to retreat and is captured by British.

December, 1776

Enlistments Due to Expire: Washington Plans Attack

The army that Washington commanded in December of 1776 was dispirited and almost broken after the disastrous events of the preceding months. The loss of New York, the hasty retreat across New Jersey, the lack of supplies, and the onset of winter all contributed to the low morale of the army on the Pennsylvania shore of the Delaware. The number of able-bodied fighting men had been reduced by almost two-thirds. To make matters worse, many enlistments would soon expire.

At the start of the Revolution the Colonists were optimistic that the war would end quickly, bringing victory and independence. Confidence was the life blood of every soldier. They believed they could easily win the war, for they were fighting on their own familiar land, while the British had to direct the war from across the Atlantic Ocean. So confident were the Colonists that enlistments during the start of the Revolution extended for only one year. On January 1, 1777 Washington would be left with almost no army if action was not taken immediately. Washington and his ragged army were temporarily safe in Pennsylvania. The British were unable to pursue them because of Washington's foresight in securing all available boats, but soon the river would be frozen and the British could again take the offensive. In the meantime Washington stationed his troops along the Delaware River from Bristol to New Hope, with the main body at Bowman's Hill (present day Washington Crossing Historic Park). From here Washington made his momentous decision to cross the Delaware River.

THOMPSON-NEELY HOUSE
Washington Crossing Historic Park, PA

The Thompson-Neely House was requisitioned from the Thompson and Neely families in December 1776 as headquarters for General Lord Stirling and his staff, which included Lieutenant James Monroe, later to become fifth president of the United States. Lord Stirling was in charge of the main body of the army camped along the Delaware to prevent a British crossing into Pennsylvania. As the headquarters of one of Washington's most trusted advisors, this would have been one of the most important outposts along the Delaware River. The Thompson-Neely House known locally as the "House of Decision" held some of the strategic conferences to develop Washington's offensive.

A gristmill stood on the property during the Revolution, grinding grain into flour for the making of bread. Tradition has it that flour for the Continental army encamped in the area was ground at the Thompson's Mill.

WASHINGTON CROSSING THE DELAWARE
An engraving after the painting by Emanuel Leutze

December 25, 1776

Washington & Army Cross Ice-Choked Delaware River

The days of December 1776 were bleak ones for Washington and what remained of his army. With the Americans forced to retreat, the British now held all of New Jersey and were perilously close to Philadelphia. Washington feared that the British force would move to take Philadelphia, putting an end to the Revolution.

December 13th Howe unexpectedly announced that the campaign was at an end and that the main body of the British army would winter in New York and resume fighting in the spring. This practice of fighting only during favorable weather was customary during the 18th century. Washington was distrustful of Howe and remained concerned that the British would attack. With few reinforcements arriving and enlistments expiring, Washington made the important decision to attack.

As part of the daring plan, Washington assembled his troops near Bowman's Hill and McConkey's Ferry. Virtually backtracking across his path of retreat, he would attempt to cross the Delaware on the night of December 25th for a surprise attack on the Hessian garrison nine miles down river at Trenton.

Three divisions would cross the river as darkness fell. Durham boats and other craft, which earlier in the month had been collected as a defensive measure, were the means of crossing. Washington, with a division of 2,400 troops under his command, crossed at McConkey's Ferry and would attack occupied Trenton from the north. The two supporting divisions did not succeed in crossing the ice-choked river. Washington's troops alone, during a blinding snowstorm, successfully made the crossing.

McCONKEY'S FERRY
Washington Crossing Historic Park, PA

In 1776 the Inn at McConkey's Ferry stood alone at the end of the road leading from Newtown to the river bank. Samuel McConkey owned the property and the innkeeper was James Brown. With earthworks and cannon defending the ferry landing, the Inn served as a guard post during the Continental army's encampment along the banks of the Delaware River that December. The McConkey Ferry Inn served as Washington's temporary headquarters on the night of the crossing. Tradition has it that General Washington and his aides ate dinner there before embarking for occupied New Jersey. Upon the army's return, the Inn was used to house Hessian officers captured at Trenton. Benjamin Taylor bought

the property in 1777. His descendents established the 19th century village of Taylorsville at what had been Taylor's Ferry from 1777 to 1835.

Washington Crossing Historic Park

Washington Crossing • Pennsylvania 18977 • 215-493-4076

Washington Crossing Historic Park, a Registered National Historic Site, was created by the Commonwealth of Pennsylvania in 1917 to "perpetuate and preserve the site on which the Continental army crossed the Delaware" on Christmas night, 1776. More than 500,000 visitors tour this foremost Bucks County attraction annually. Major exhibits include the exact copy of the famous Leutze painting, "Washington Crossing the Delaware," and a Durham boat barn containing four replicas of the cargo craft used by Washington in the crossing. At the embarkation point, the McConkey Ferry Inn dating back to the time of the crossing still stands. Across from the Inn a large statue depicts the Leutze painting.

Five miles north of the Memorial Building is the Thompson-Neely area of the park. The Thompson-Neely House, headquarters of General Stirling during December, 1776, played an important role in the events leading to the crossing of the Delaware. The restored house now features furnished rooms and exhibits. Here may be found the unique Bowman's Hill Wildflower Preserve consisting of about 100 acres of woods, wildflowers, and nature trails which preserve plants native to Pennsylvania. The preserve was established to commemorate the site of the encampment of Washington's troops in 1776. Bowman's Hill itself was used as a lookout point by Washington's men. Bowman's Hill Tower, built in 1930, was reopened in 1985 after extensive renovation.

The historic crossing of 1776 gives Christmas Day an additional patriotic meaning which is particularly American. Each Christmas afternoon, hundreds participate in the re-enactment of Washington crossing the Delaware in Durham boats in a ceremony attracting thousands.

The park is administered jointly by the Pennsylvania Historical and Museum Commission and the Washington Crossing Park Commission, with the assistance of the Bowman's Hill Wildflower Preserve Association and the Washington Crossing Foundation.

RESOURCES

Restored and furnished 18th and 19th Century buildings; Durham boats; special events; recreational area; wildflower preserve.

MEMORIAL BUILDING/VISITOR CENTER

Reproduction *Washington Crossing the Delaware* painting by Emanuel Leutze with narration, film, exhibits, library, and shop.

EDUCATIONAL PROGRAMS

Educational material for school group visits is being developed. Call for information. The 28 minute film *Washington Crossing the Delaware* is shown at the Memorial Building throughout the day (call for schedule). Copies are available for purchase or rent in film or video cassette format. Contact the Washington Crossing Foundation for information, 215-493-6577.

TOUR INFORMATION

Start at the Memorial Building to see the Leutze painting of *Washington Crossing The Delaware* accompanied by a brief narration. Guided tours of the historic buildings are available. Groups are required to make reservations in advance. Tickets and a brochure guide are available here.

LIBRARY

The Washington Crossing Library of the American Revolution is located in the Memorial Building. The library contains a collection of books and manuscripts about the American Revolution. Call for an appointment.

FOOD SERVICE

Picnic area available. Picnic pavilions available for groups, call for reservations. Food facilities near park.

ADMISSION

Memorial Building free. Admission for historic buildings: adults $1.50; seniors $1.00; children $.50; organized school groups free. Additional admission for observation tower.

HOURS

Monday—Saturday, 9:00 a.m. to 5:00 p.m. Sunday, Noon to 5:00 p.m.

LOCATION & PARKING

McConkey's Ferry area & Memorial Building/Visitor Center on Pennsylvania Route 32 and Route 532, between Yardley and New Hope; Thompson-Neely area 5 miles north on Route 32. Vehicle and bus parking on park grounds.

Washington Crossing the Delaware

Many of the enlisted men and officers, including George Washington, wrote about their daily experiences during the Revolutionary War in diaries. These diaries were written because many wanted to keep a record of the important events of the Revolution. Also, writing a diary helped to pass the lonely hours spent far away from home and family fighting for independence. These diaries offer us an important personal point of view of the Revolution.

Diary Account by Captain Thomas Forrest,
an Officer on Washington's staff.

December 25, 1776.
Christmas, 6 P.M.

The regiments have had their evening parade, but instead of returning to their quarters are marching toward the ferry. It is fearfully cold and raw and a snow-storm setting in. The wind is north-east and beats in the faces of the men. It will be a terrible night for the soldiers who have no shoes. Some of them have tied old rags around their feet; others are barefoot, but I have not heard a man complain. They are ready to suffer any hardship and die rather than give up their liberty.

Instructions

Imagine yourself as a boatman on December 25, 1776, the eve of the Battle of Trenton. As a member of John Glover's regiment of sailors and fishermen from Marblehead, Massachusetts it is your responsibility to transport the army across the Delaware River in a Durham boat before the battle. Write a diary account of your crossing. Include the following details in your account: you must transport men, horses, cannons, and supplies across the river in your 60 foot Durham boat; you cross in the middle of the night during a severe rain and sleet storm; you use long poles to propel your craft across the ice-filled Delaware River; you will have to make many trips during the night.

December 25, 1776

At McConkey's Ferry, Pennsylvania

Private ______________________

of John Glover's Massachusetts Regiment

December 26, 1776

Washington Marshals Army March to Trenton Begins

Durham boats, ferry boats, and other water craft were employed to transport Washington's army and equipment across the Delaware River from McConkey's Ferry on the Pennsylvania side to Johnson's Ferry on the New Jersey shore. The current carried the loaded Durham boats downstream while a crew of three to six men navigated and poled each boat across.

On the night of December 25th-26th, 1776, nine laborious hours were required to transport Washington's army, cannon, horses, powder, shot, and wagons across the Delaware River to the New Jersey shore. Only the troops under Washington's command succeeded in crossing; the two corps under the command of Lieutenant Colonel John Cadwalader and Brigadier General James Ewing were unable to cross and aid in the attack. The crossing, scheduled to begin at 4:00 p.m. and be completed by midnight, was hampered by bitter cold, severe rain and snow, and ice floating in the river. Hopelessly behind schedule, Washington's surprise attack at dawn was impossible.

At Johnson's Ferry Washington marshaled his troops for the nine mile march to Trenton. Major General Nathanael Greene's corps, accompanied by Washington, led the march toward Trenton via the Pennington Road. Major General John Sullivan's corps took the Old River Road. The plan required the two corps to attack Trenton from two points, a pincer maneuver. Despite the delays and severe weather, Washington remained undaunted in his efforts to take Trenton.

JOHNSON FERRY HOUSE
Washington Crossing State Park, NJ

The first American troops to view Johnson's Ferry House on the east bank of the Delaware River Christmas night, 1776 were a company of Virginia riflemen instructed to form a cordon around the landing site. A Captain Fitzgerald noted in his diary in Johnson's Ferry House at 3:00 a.m., December 26, 1776, that General Washington was standing on the Jersey shore of the Delaware, wrapped in his warm black cloak, watching the landing of the last of the troops. It would be 4:00 a.m. before the last boatload got across with the men and their supplies.

It is doubtful that Johnson's Ferry House has ever witnessed a busier or more hectic evening in its history than that of Christmas, 1776.

Washington Crossing State Park

Box 337-A, R.D. # 1 • Titusville, New Jersey 08560 • 609-737-9303

Washington Crossing State Park is located along the banks of the Delaware River in Mercer County, New Jersey. The Park commemorates the site where the American Continental army, commanded by George Washington, made the historic river crossing on Christmas night, 1776.

The State Park, established in 1912, contains 807 acres and extends about one mile east from the historic river bank. Continental Lane over which the American troops marched on Christmas night, 1776 extends nearly the full length of the Park, offering visitors the opportunity to walk along the same path as Washington and his army. A number of historical memorials have been installed by patriotic and similar organizations along the lane.

The park features numerous historic structures. The Johnson Ferry House is a historic landmark from the American Revolutionary era. The original portion of the house was constructed in 1740 by Rut Johnson and consisted of the two downstairs front rooms and the upstairs loft. When the Johnson family grew in size, an addition was placed onto the house, including the rear rooms of the first and second floors. At the time of the historic crossing, the house was the homestead for the James Slack family who were the ferry operators.

The Nelson House, located in Washington grove west of State Route #29, consists of a small fieldstone house once part of a large hotel operated by the Nelson family. It now houses a small museum featuring exhibits depicting the history of water transportation and a museum shop and bookstore.

The Colonial Barn Museum, located opposite the Johnson Ferry House, presents dioramas of miniature soldiers crossing the Delaware and the key battles during the "Ten Crucial Days" of 1776 and 1777.

RESOURCES

Visitor center: exhibits of Revolutionary War artifacts; audio-visual programs; park information; restored ferry house; nature center; open air theatre; special events.

VISITOR CENTER

The important events that took place during the "Ten Crucial Days," December 25, 1776 to January 3, 1777, are highlighted in the exhibits and audio-visual programs presented at the Visitor Center. The Swan Collection of the American Revolution, an extensive collection of Revolutionary artifacts, is on exhibit here. Visitors should begin their tour here to receive background information before exploring the park.

EDUCATIONAL PROGRAMS

Films on the American Revolution are available on request for viewing by scheduled groups at the Visitor Center. Advance arrangements required. Call for reservations.

TOUR INFORMATION

The audio-visual orientation program prepares groups and individuals for a more meaningful tour of the park. Guided tours of the exhibit area are available for groups with advance reservations. Visitors may tour the exhibits on a self-guided basis. Staff members are available to answer questions. Guided nature tours are available for groups with advance reservations. Tours of the park's historic buildings and grounds are on a self-guided basis. Call for reservations: Visitor Center, 609-737-9303; Nature Center, 609-737-0609.

FOOD SERVICE

Extensive picnic facilities are available throughout the park. Groups of 20 or more may reserve specific picnic facilities in advance. Call the park office for reservations, 609-737-0623.

ADMISSION

$1.00 per vehicle weekends and holidays during summer months.

HOURS

Visitor's Center: 9:00 a.m. to 5:00 p.m. daylight saving time, 9:00 a.m. to 4:30 p.m. standard time.

LOCATION & PARKING

Park Entrance on County Route 546 near NJ State Route 29, nine miles north of Trenton. Adequate vehicle and bus parking in park.

From the Collection of the New Jersey State Museum

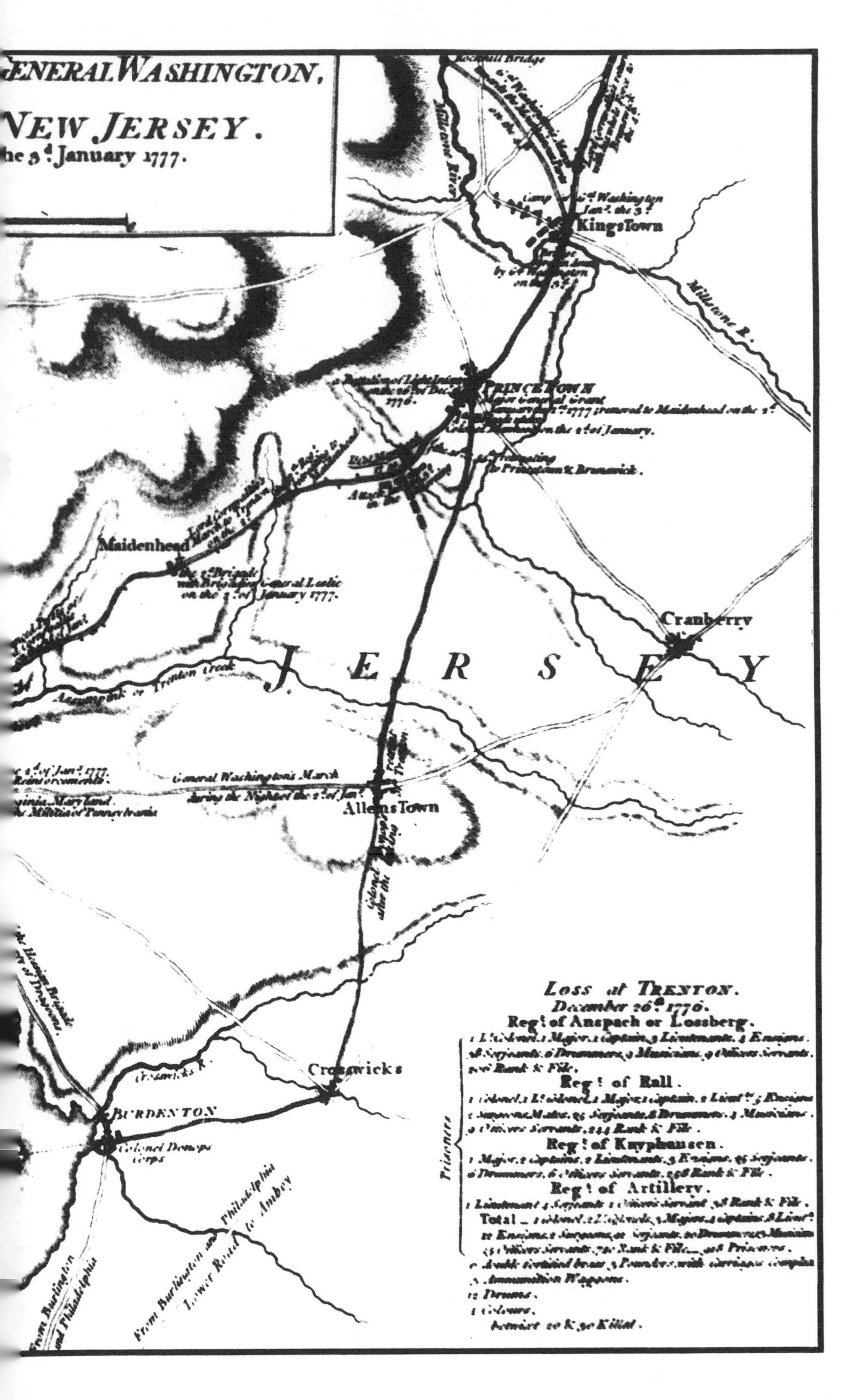
GENERAL WASHINGTON,
NEW JERSEY.
the 3d January 1777.
Millstone River
KingsTown
Millstone R.
PRINCETOWN
Maidenhead
Cranberry
JERSEY
Assunpink or Trenton Creek
General Washington's March
during the Night of the 2d of Jan.
AllensTown
Crosswicks
BURDENTON
Colonel Donops corps
From Burlington and Philadelphia
Lower Road to Amboy
Loss at TRENTON.
December 26th 1776.
Regt of Anspach or Loosberg.
Regt of Rall.
Regt of Knyphausen.
Regt of Artillery.
Total
Prisoners
Ammunition Waggons.
12 Drums.
Killed.

December 26, 1776, *Newport, RI*
British establish a strong naval base in New England.

December 27, 1776, *Baltimore, MD*
Congress grants Washington dictatorial powers over military affairs.

December 27, 1776, *Johnson's Ferry, NJ*
Washington, army, and captured Hessians recross Delaware River to Pennsylvania.

December 26, 1776

Americans Victorious at Trenton Hessian Soldiers Captured

The city of Trenton, and the Old Barracks, were occupied by Colonel Johann Gottlieb Rall and the 1,586 Hessian mercenary troops in his command. Rall felt secure against any attack by the American force, which he referred to as "nothing but a lot of farmers." The British forces, along with their Hessian allies, assumed the fighting was over for the winter, so they made few attempts to secure their positions in New Jersey. Trenton was no exception. Located on flat country and accessible from many roads, Trenton was protected on the west only by the Delaware River. Redoubts were to have been constructed around Trenton, but Colonel Rall failed to order their completion.

At 8 a.m. on the 26th, Washington's men engaged a Hessian guard outside Trenton, and the battle began. The sleeping Hessians were taken by surprise, but they quickly assembled in the streets in an attempt to defend the garrison. The battle raged on in the city streets for two hours through snow, sleet, hail, and rain. The American attack forced Rall to order his troops to withdraw to an apple orchard just outside town. In the orchard, Rall was fatally wounded, and the Hessians were surrounded and forced to surrender. The Americans emerged victorious at a most critical time. As Sir George Otto Trevelyan, eminent British historian, wrote of these events: "It may be doubted whether so small a number of men ever employed so short a space of time with greater and more lasting results upon the history of the world."

OLD BARRACKS
Trenton, New Jersey

The Old Barracks was built by New Jersey's colonial assembly to house British troops in 1758, eighteen years before the Battle of Trenton. A barracks is a large building designed to house soldiers. Five barracks were built in New Jersey to house troops protecting British settlers during the French and Indian Wars.

At the time of the Revolution, armies usually fought only during the warmer months, wintering in barracks, private homes, or encampments. During the winter of 1776 the Old Barracks housed some of the Hessian troops stationed in Trenton, their families, and New Jersey residents loyal to the King of England. The rest of the force resided in private homes in the village. After the battle the American forces used the barracks to house troops, and through much of the war it was used as a military hospital.

Old Barracks Museum

Barrack Street • Trenton, New Jersey 08608 • 609-396-1776

Today the Barracks and the adjacent "Officers' Quarters" form a museum complex devoted to interpreting life during the days before and after the Revolution. Located in the heart of Trenton, visitors coming from the hustle and bustle of the city are imaginatively carried back to the 18th century when they enter the Old Barracks. Visitors meet and interact with characters from the past—a soldier, camp followers, elegant ladies, and farmers' wives.

The Trenton barracks was one of five built in New Jersey in 1758 with funds appropriated by the Colonial legislature. Only the Trenton barracks stands as a reminder of New Jersey's place in the colonial struggles of the New World. It is the only original barracks still standing in North America dating from the French and Indian Wars.

After the Revolution the barracks was sold and divided into private homes. When Trenton was made the state capital in 1790 and a site was chosen near the barracks for the State House, the "old" barracks became a valuable property. In 1793 the middle section of the barracks was torn down so that Front Street could run uninterrupted to the State House.

Many families lived in the small apartments in the two parts of the original barracks, separated by Front Street. The interior and exterior of the building underwent extensive change. The building was advertised for sale in 1899, but few recognized its historic significance. Fearing that it might not survive the wrecker's ball, a group of civic-minded women from Trenton formed the Purchase Fund Committee in order to buy the building and preserve it for future generations. Because of their efforts the Old Barracks stands today as a Registered State and National Historic Landmark.

RESOURCES

Restored 18th century barracks: museum; period rooms; gallery spaces; audio-visual program; museum shop; special events.

EDUCATIONAL PROGRAMS

Educational workshops for school groups can be scheduled to complement a tour — *A Soldier's Life, Colonial Home-Life, Style in the Eighteenth Century*, and colonial craft programs. Costumed staff members are available to visit area classrooms to present *A Soldier's Life* or *Colonial Home-Life. The Spirit of 1776*, a dramatized school assembly program is also offered. Craft workshops for adults are scheduled regularly. A variety of educational materials are available free of charge to school groups. Call for information and reservations.

TOUR INFORMATION

A slide/tape program introduces the visitor to the Old Barracks. The guided tour of the Barracks includes information on its history, collections, and social history of the 18th century. A special program is offered to school groups with advance reservations. School groups are escorted through the Barracks where they encounter costumed interpreters representing people from the past. Students participate in "hands-on" activities. This program is currently being adapted for the general public.

FOOD SERVICE

A brown bag lunchroom is available to groups with reservations.

ADMISSION

Adults $ 1.00; children 12 & under $ .50;
senior citizen groups & educational groups free.

HOURS

Monday—Saturday, 10:00 a.m. to 5:00 p.m., Sundays, 1:00 p.m. to 5:00 p.m.

Closed Thanksgiving, December 24th & 25th, New Year's & Easter.

LOCATION & PARKING

Located in the heart of Trenton, immediately south of and adjacent to the State Capitol Building. Metered parking is available on W. State St.; parking garage on Front St. On weekends use the Capitol Building parking lot.

ADDITIONAL SITES

The Trenton Battle Monument marks the site of the American artillery during the Battle of Trenton. The monument is located at "Five Points"; the intersection of N. Broad St., Warren St., Brunswick Ave., Pennington Ave., and Princeton Ave. For information call 609-737-0623.

Uniforms of the American Revolution

British soldiers were called "Red Coats" during the American Revolution because they wore red wool jackets. Unlike the British troops, the American army lacked a standard uniform for its men. Shortages of materials and supplies forced officers to clothe their men with what was available. American troops wore blue, brown, green, and even red jackets during the Revolution. Many of the men lacked uniforms altogether and wore civilian clothes. Many regiments attempted to clothe their men in the same style and color uniforms. This practice aided the men in recognizing fellow soldiers from enemy soldiers during battle.

Instructions

The wool regimental jacket was usually of one color with the facings (collar, cuffs, and lapels) of another color. The following are colors adapted by the American, British and Hessian forces during the Revolution. Using the chart below, color and label each soldier on the accompanying illustration. On the extra American soldier design a color scheme of your own.

MILITARY UNIFORM COLORS

	COAT	FACINGS	BREECHES (pants)
Continental Marines	Green	White	Buff
Continental Army, 12th Regiment	Brown	Red	Buff
Colonel Henley's Continental Regiment	Red	Light Blue	White
Pennsylvania Line, 5th Regiment	Blue	White	Red
Hessian Grenadier, Regiment Von Rall	Blue	Red	Buff
British Infantry, 47th Regiment	Red	White	Buff

Soldiers of the Revolution

Hessian

British

Continental

Continental

Continental

Continental

Continental

December 30, 1777

Americans Recross Delaware River & Occupy Trenton

With the overwhelming victory at Trenton, morale was restored among the American forces, but Washington and his men remained in a difficult situation. Washington feared that as long as he remained in Trenton, his army was vulnerable to attack by the British forces in New Jersey. Therefore, after the victory at Trenton, the army marched the nine miles up the Delaware River to the site of its historic crossing and recrossed the Delaware River into the safety of Pennsylvania.

Washington was determined to try to force the British from New Jersey, but time was running out for him. Enlistments would expire at the end of December, and his army would be dangerously reduced. In an effort to maintain the army, Washington offered a $10.00 bounty in silver to men who would extend their enlistments for an additional six weeks. These efforts, along with the victory at Trenton, brought new recruits from Philadelphia and gave Washington the forces to launch another attack. After the Battle of Trenton, the British consolidated their forces in Princeton. Washington recrossed the ice-filled Delaware and occupied Trenton again.

The British were enraged at Washington's daring attack and victory at Trenton and vowed not to abandon New Jersey. Lord Cornwallis was given command of the British forces there and arrived in Princeton the night of January 1st to take command. He immediately called a council of war and determined that the following morning the British would march on Trenton.

New Jersey & the Revolution — *Additional Sites*

NASSAU HALL
PRINCETON UNIVERSITY

Nassau Hall was the site of many significant events during the Revolution. It served as a barracks and hospital for Continental and British troops, the site of the last stand by the British in the Battle of Princeton, the home of the first Legislature of the State of New Jersey, and the home of the Continental Congress from June to November 1783. Although the building has undergone extensive redesign and reconstruction, visitors can still get a sense of the important events that took place here.

One hour tours of Nassau Hall and the campus are available through Orange Key Guide Service located in the John Maclean House to the right of Nassau Hall. Self-guided tours are also allowed.

MORVEN
Princeton, NJ

Morven was the 18th Century home of Richard Stockton, a signer of the Declaration of Independence. Adjacent to Morven stands the Princeton Battle Monument.

Morven is operated by the New Jersey Historical Society. Tours are available for individuals and groups. Call for schedule information and reservation, 609-683-1755.

A Death at the Battle of Princeton

At the Field of Action near Princeton
Sunday Evening Jany. 5th [1777]

My Dr. Friend

Tho the Acct. I send is a melancholy one (in one respect) yet I have sent an express to give you the best information I can collect. Our mutual Friend Anthony Morris died here in three Hours after he received his Wounds on Friday morning; They were three in Number, one on his Chin, one on the Knee & the third & fatal one on the right Temple, by a grapeshot. Brave Man! he fought and died nobly, deserving a much better fate. General Mercer is dangerously ill indeed. I have scarce any hopes of him, the Villians have stab'd him five different Places. The dead on our Side at this Place amount to sixteen, that of the Enemy to 23. They have retreated to Brunswick with the greatest Precipitation, and from Accounts just come, the Hero Washington is not far from them; they never have been so shamefully drub'd and out general'd in every Respect; I hourly expect to hear of their whole Army being cut to pieces or made Prisoners.

From a letter by Jonathan Potts to Owen Biddle.

January 3, 1777

Americans on the Offensive: British Defeated at Princeton

Washington's meager force stationed in Trenton on January 2nd was far outnumbered by the approaching force of over 6,000 well-trained British troops. The only hope for the Americans was to concentrate their forces and to outmaneuver the British. Washington ordered the troops in Allentown and Bordentown to Trenton, and set up a strong defensive line outside Trenton to block the enemy's approach from Princeton. On January 2nd the approaching British force met the Americans. The Americans succeeded in delaying the British approach to Trenton throughout the day, but by dusk the British advance guard pushed into the city. They were met by heavy American artillery fire along the Assunpink Creek. The British brought up their own artillery, but they were unable to break the American line. Washington successfully protected his main force from the British attack, but he feared that the British would resume the fight at daybreak.

That evening Washington held a council of war to establish his next move. Washington found himself in a difficult situation, but he remained unwilling to retreat. Outnumbered by the main British force poised to attack, Washington and his army outmaneuvered the British. Leaving several hundred New Jersey militia to stoke the campfires, Washington and the rest of the army secretly slipped out of camp during the night. Washington planned to attack the three British garrisons stationed in Princeton at dawn. The British were fooled by Washington's ruse and remained unaware of the danger to their force in Princeton.

CLARKE HOUSE PRINCETON BATTLEFIELD STATE PARK

Princeton, New Jersey

At dawn the Americans were only three miles from Princeton. The British force at Princeton, unaware of the presence of the American army in the area, began a march toward Trenton to reinforce the main "attacking force." As the British force was marching out of town, the American advance guard, commanded by General Hugh Mercer, was marching into town. Within minutes the opposing forces became aware of each other. As both forces maneuvered for position, they accidentally met in an orchard. Mercer's men fought valiantly even though outnumbered by the British. The ensuing battle ended favorably for the Americans only after the arrival of Washington and the main American force. Washington's personal bravery halted the fleeing troops and secured the victory. The British retreated into the town itself, taking up a defensive position in Nassau Hall. After a few rounds of artillery fire, they quickly surrendered.

The Thomas Clarke House
Princeton Battlefield State Park

500 Mercer Street • Princeton, New Jersey 08540 • 609-921-0074

The Thomas Clarke House is located in Princeton Battlefield State Park. The Park commemorates the historic Battle of Princeton, fought on January 3, 1777, at which General Washington led the American forces to victory. This battlefield is one of the few to remain virtually unchanged since the Revolution.

Thomas Clarke was a Quaker farmer who acquired two hundred acres of land in 1770 which had been in the Clarke family since 1696. He then built the house today known as the Clarke House. After his death in 1802, the house and property were inherited by Thomas' brother Ezekiel. The house remained in the Clarke family until 1863, when it was sold to Henry E. Hale. It has changed owners only twice since then. In 1946 the State of New Jersey purchased the house and the surrounding land for a State park.

In the intense fighting near the Clarke House during the Battle of Princeton, General Hugh Mercer of the Continental army received seven bayonet wounds. Refusing to be carried from the field until victory was certain, he was laid under an oak tree, which still stands in the Park. He was later carried to the Clarke House where he was cared for by the Clarke family and several surgeons. After nine days he died of his wounds. In recognition of his dedication to the freedom of the Colonies, Mercer County was later named in his honor.

The original portion of the Clarke House stands today faced with white clapboards. It has remained unchanged, and it consists of two stories containing six rooms that are now furnished with period pieces and that are open to the public. Nearby are a smoke house and a carriage shed. The house was restored in 1975 and first opened to the public on July 4, 1976.

RESOURCES

Restored & furnished 18th century house; battleground park; special events.

TOUR INFORMATION

A staff member or volunteer guides groups or individuals through the Clarke House on a 15 to 30 minute tour. Tours are limited to 25 per group. Advance reservations required for group tours. Self-guided tours of the house are not available. A special program on the Battle of Princeton is available on request. Call for reservations.

FOOD SERVICE

Picnicking is allowed on the grounds, but no shelter or tables are available.

ADMISSION

Free

HOURS

Wednesday—Friday, 9:00 a.m. to Noon & 1:00 p.m. to 5:00 p.m. Saturday, 10:00 a.m. to Noon & 1:00 p.m. to 5:00 p.m. Sunday, 1:00 p.m. to 5:00 p.m.
Site closes at dusk in fall and winter.

LOCATION & PARKING

Route 583 south of Princeton, NJ. Vehicle and bus parking on park grounds.

January 6, 1777, *Morristown, NJ*
Washington and 5,000 troops arrive in Morristown for the winter.

February 23, 1777, *Amboy, NJ*
A British foraging expedition of 4,000 is blocked by Americans.

March 5, 1777, *Philadelphia, PA*
British are no longer a threat: Congress returns to Philadelphia.

January 6 - May 28, 1777

Victorious Army to Winter in Morristown, NJ

During the preceding "ten crucial days," December 25th to January 3rd, Washington through his courage and determination was able to change the course of the Revolution from one of defeat to one of victory for the American cause. His efforts at Trenton and Princeton forced the British to abandon New Jersey, once again putting a safe distance between the British force and the patriot capital of Philadelphia. Washington gathered his weary troops at Princeton and marched into winter quarters at Morristown on January 6th. Washington could hardly have picked a more defensible place in which to rest and reassemble his army. The Watchung Mountains to the east protected him from Howe's army in New York City, only 30 miles away. The mountain passes could easily be defended, and lookouts posted on ridge tops could quickly spy any British move on Morristown or Philadelphia. Seeing that his army was safely quartered, Washington used the winter lull to fill his ranks and forge them into a more effective fighting force.

The exhausted troops arrived in Morristown and found a few buildings clustered around the town green — a large open field often used for grazing sheep, cattle, and horses. The Presbyterian and Baptist churches dominated the scene, while the courthouse and jail served the legal needs of the town and surrounding farm communities. Much of the town's social, political, and business life was conducted at Jacob Arnold's tavern, Washington's headquarter's in 1777.

MORRISTOWN NATIONAL HISTORICAL PARK
Morristown, New Jersey

In the surrounding countryside prosperous farmers raised wheat, corn, rye, oats, barley, vegetables, apples, peaches, and other fruits. Much of the land was heavily forested. In the hills north of Morristown mines and furnaces yielded pig iron, which was cast into tools, farm implements and cannon at the forges of Hibernia and Mt. Hope.

Maintaining the size and efficiency of the army was a continuing problem. The force began to dwindle as enlistments expired, and many of the men deserted. In an attempt to gain new recruits, Washington sent every officer that he could spare back to his home state on a recruiting drive.

Replacements slowly trickled in, but these were often local militia and raw recruits. Many of the replacements were resistant to military discipline, and they often damaged their cause by harassing the farmers of the countryside.

Morristown National Historical Park

Washington Place • Morristown, New Jersey 07960 • 201-539-2085

Washington and his Army spent two winters encamped in Morristown. In addition to the 1777 encampment, the winter of '79-'80 brought Washington and nearly 12,000 troops to Morristown. Most of the remnants of the first encampment are gone, but a great deal remains from the second encampment as a reminder of the ordeal the men suffered during one of the most severe winters of the century.

The Ford Mansion, a model of Georgian architecture, served as Washington's headquarters and command post during the winter of '79-'80. During this period, the house served as quarters for Washington, his aides and servants, and his wife Martha who joined him whenever possible, as well as the Ford family and their servants. Today the house is furnished as it would have been during this period of the Revolution.

The bulk of the 12,000 troops spent the winter of '79-'80 at nearby Jockey Hollow. Nearly nine hundred acres of timber were cleared and used to construct 1,200 log huts to protect the men from the severe weather. The huts measured 14 feet wide, 16 feet long, and 6.5 feet high and housed twelve men who slept in wooden bunks. These crudely constructed soldiers' huts served as temporary housing, and none has lasted to the present day. The park has reconstructed and equipped several huts to give the modern day visitor a sense of the Revolutionary encampment.

Morristown National Historical Park is divided into two major areas approximately six miles apart. Washington's Headquarters area, located in the center of Morristown, features the Museum, Library, and Ford Mansion. Seven miles southwest is the Jockey Hollow area which features a visitor's center, encampment site with reconstructed soldiers' huts, and the Wick House and orchard.

RESOURCES
Restored 18th century buildings; encampment site with reconstructed soldiers' huts; special events.

MUSEUM
Located at Washington's Headquarters. Exhibits of military equipment, furniture & decorative arts; interpretive film & audio-visual program; museum shop & bookstore.

VISITOR CENTER
Located at Jockey Hollow. Audio-visual program, interpretive exhibits including a full scale replica of a soldiers' hut; museum shop & bookstore.

EDUCATIONAL PROGRAMS
An outstanding full day program is available to school groups with advance reservations. Park rangers and costumed interpreters escort the group to all major areas and buildings on site. Emphasis is on military, community, and social life during the Revolution. Outreach programs are available on a limited basis. Call for information and reservations.

TOUR INFORMATION
Tours of the park can begin at either the headquarters building or the visitor center. Rangers and costumed interpreters are stationed throughout the park to aid self-guided visitors. Brochures and a park handbook are available. Group tours and programs for the handicapped are available with advance reservations.

LIBRARY
An extensive research library featuring original books, manuscripts and other material on the Colonial and Revolutionary War periods of American history is housed in Washington's Headquarters Museum. Call for information, 201-539-2016.

FOOD SERVICE
Picnicking is available only at the Lewis Morris County Park located near the soldiers' hut area of Jockey Hollow.

ADMISSION
Adults $ .50; seniors & children free; group tours free.

HOURS
Daily, 9:00 a.m. to 5:00 p.m.
Closed Thanksgiving, Christmas, & New Year's Day.

LOCATION & PARKING
Jockey Hollow Encampment Area, I-287, exit 26B; Washington's Headquarters Area & Museum, I-287 & Route 510 in Morristown.

March 14, 1777, *Morristown, NJ*
Army reduced to 3,000 due to expired enlistments and desertion.

May 21, 1777, *Morristown, NJ*
New recruits increase American force to 10,000 officers and men.

May 28, 1777, *Morristown, NJ*
Army leaves Morristown to block the British force from Philadelphia.

Winter 1777

Washington Inoculates Army Against Smallpox

The 5,000 men who arrived in Morristown from Princeton during the winter of 1777 sought shelter from the blasts of winter in any available structure. Adequate housing for the entire army was not available in Morristown, which consisted only of 50 or 60 buildings. Public buildings, private homes, stables, barns, sheds, and tents were all used to house the men. Because of the shortage of adequate housing and the need to secure the area while keeping a watchful eye on British troop movements, the majority of the American troops were spread throughout the mountains to guard all approaches to Morristown. Washington remained headquartered in the town itself throughout the winter with a small guard and staff.

Disease added yet another burden to the army's struggles to survive. Smallpox, "the greatest of all calamities," struck the small army, and Washington had to resort to desperate measures to maintain the health of his men. At a time when the procedure was feared and almost as dangerous as the disease itself, Washington who had himself suffered from smallpox, ordered both soldiers and civilians to be inoculated against smallpox.

In spite of these difficulties, and the ever-present shortages of food and clothing, the army kept fighting. Small units waylaid enemy foraging parties, cut off supplies, and attacked the British in countless skirmishes. Supplies vital to both American and British armies often became the object of minor engagements. Captured food found its way back to the American camps and often made the difference between starvation and survival.

Washington's Optimism at Morristown

Morristown

The Enemy, by [our] two lucky Strokes at Trenton and Princeton, have been obliged to abandon every part of Jersey, except Brunswick and Amboy and the small tract of Country between them, which is so intirely exhausted of Supplies of every kind, that I hope, by preventing them from sending their foraging Parties to any great distance, to reduce them to the utmost distress, in the course of this Winter.

From a letter by George Washington to Maj. Gen. Philip Shuyler.

Pastimes of the Revolutionary Soldier

Soldiers in camp spent their spare time in many ways. Torn uniforms were in constant need of repair, and a soldier quickly learned to sew. Whittling not only helped to pass the time, but it provided the soldier with many useful items such as cups, mugs, and cooking utensils. Games such as backgammon and darts, which remain popular today, were played in the camps. It was not unusual for soldiers to have their families with them in camp. The men often made toys for their children. One popular 18th century plaything was the humdinger or buzz toy.

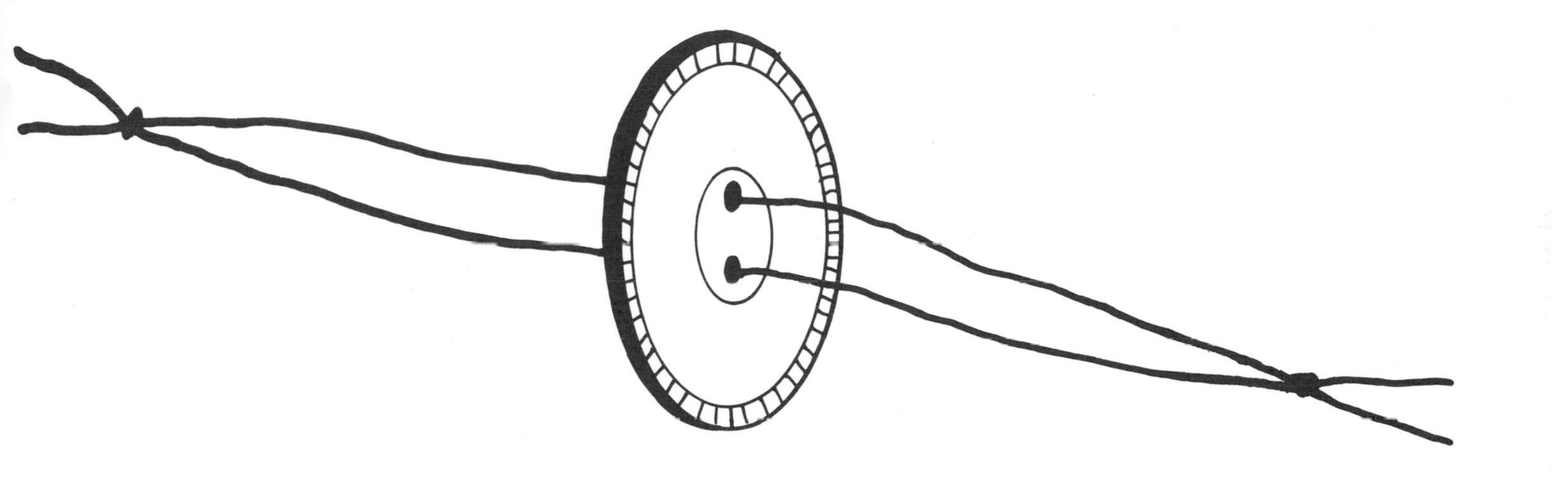

Instructions

To make a humdinger of your own you will need:

1 large button (about two inches in diameter)

2 pieces of string each two feet long

Thread each piece of string through opposite holes in the button and knot the ends together.

To operate, slip the knots over the middle finger of each hand. With your hands about 18" apart, move them in a circular motion away from you. This action will twist the cords together. When the string is wound up pull your hands apart quickly to start the button spinning. When the string is completely stretched out, relax your hands so the button keeps twirling, winding the string up again. Continue pulling and relaxing as long as you like. The humdinger should produce a humming noise while it is spinning.

Early humdingers were often made from a round wooden or bone disk, or a metal coin.

June 14, 1777

Congress Passes Flag Resolution: Stars & Stripes

Before the Declaration of Independence, the Colonists flew the flag of Great Britain as loyal citizens of the crown. Once the movement toward independence had begun, a flag symbolizing this break and proclaiming the union of the thirteen Colonies was necessary. During the early days of the Revolution, the "Grand Union" Flag was used. It consisted of thirteen red and white stripes symbolizing the states of the new nation and the British Union flag in the upper left-hand corner symbolizing the Colonists' hope of reconciling their differences with Britain. As the Revolution progressed, a variety of flag designs were used and popularized by various states and military regiments.

On June 14, 1777 Congress passed a resolution recognizing the design of a flag for the new nation. Congress "Resolved that the Flag of the thirteen United States be 13 stripes alternate red and white, that the Union be 13 stars white in a blue field representing a new constellation." Perhaps they had seen the thirteen stripe flag with thirteen stars in a circle which appears in contemporary paintings and which is ascribed to Betsy Ross. The Congressional resolution being vague, many flags with different star arrangements appeared. The five point star was widely used, but stars of six to eight points were also used. After the Revolution, as new states were formed, stripes as well as stars were added to the flag. It was not until July 4, 1818 that Congress returned the flag to its original thirteen stripes and provided for the addition of a star to symbolize each state.

BETSY ROSS HOUSE
Philadelphia, Pennsylvania

Betsy Ross lived in Philadelphia during the Revolution in a modest row house that she shared with her family and worked as a seamstress. Many colonists devoted an area of their homes to the family trade or business. The Ross house is a typical example of this. Betsy and her husband, John Ross, established an upholsterer's shop in their home. Betsy maintained the shop after John Ross was killed in 1776 in a munitions explosion. Betsy performed upholstery work for Benjamin Franklin, the Society of Free Quakers, and the State House of Pennsylvania.

Oral tradition has it that Betsy Ross made the first American flag, and to date no firm evidence disproving this claim exists. As a patriot, Betsy Ross did make flags for the Pennsylvania Navy and musket balls for the Continental army, aiding the War effort as she could.

Betsy Ross House

239 Arch Street • Philadelphia, Pennsylvania 19106 • 215-627-5343

The Betsy Ross House, located in Old City Philadelphia, is furnished to reflect Betsy Ross' full and varied life. The house is divided into living and working areas, typical of many middle class homes of the eighteenth century. The craft of the seamstress and upholsterer is presented at the site, in addition to an area devoted to the production of musket balls which Betsy made for the Continental army. Family life was carried on in the other areas of the house. Visitors can tour the restored parlor, bed chambers, and the multi-purpose basement kitchen. Many items on display were owned by Betsy Ross, including a highboy, chairs, spectacles, a snuff box, and a family Bible. The Betsy Ross house is unique in that it is furnished to allow the visitor to experience the life of a patriotic Philadelphia woman who contributed much to our American heritage.

RESOURCES
Restored and furnished Eighteenth Century Philadelphia row house.

VISITOR CENTER
Museum shop and bookstore; food concession.

TOUR INFORMATION
Individuals and groups may tour the house on a self-guided basis. Each room depicts an aspect of work and family life associated with Betsy Ross. Interpretive labels aid the visitor. A small yard adjacent to the house offers visitors a quiet resting place in the heart of busy Philadelphia.

FOOD SERVICE
A concession is available behind the house in the visitor center.

ADMISSION
Free

HOURS
Daily, 9:00 a.m. to 6:00 p.m. May—October, 9:00 a.m. to 5:00 p.m. November—April. Closed Thanksgiving, Christmas & New Year's Day.

LOCATION & PARKING
239 Arch Street, between Second & Third Streets, Old City section of Philadelphia. Parking is not available at the site. Vehicle & bus parking 125 Second Street between Chestnut & Walnut Streets.

Stars and Stripes

American Revolutionary Flag

Instructions

Flags served as symbols of the patriots' determination to secure independence from Britain. Many of the symbols, such as stars and stripes, have remained popular to this day. Others, such as the rattlesnake and pine tree, are no longer used. In the space provided design an American Revolutionary flag of your own. Use symbols that are meaningful to you.

Pine Tree Flag of New England

Naval Flag of South Carolina with rattlesnake

Grand Union Flag with thirteen stripes

American Revolutionary Flag
Designed by

____

June & July, 1777

Troops On the Move: Philadelphia - British Goal

Although deterred by the successful American campaign of 1776-'77, British Commander-in-Chief General Sir William Howe remained determined to take Philadelphia. Headquartered in New York City, Howe decided to move his army by sea to Philadelphia. Washington had no way of knowing with certainty that Philadelphia was Howe's goal or that he planned a sea approach, so he remained prepared for both a land or sea attack. During May and June of 1777, the two armies maneuvered in northern New Jersey engaging in minor skirmishes. Howe hoped to force Washington into a major confrontation while preparations for the sea voyage were being made, but Washington remained cautious and failed to fall into the trap.

Howe gathered 15,000 men for the voyage to Philadelphia. On July 23rd, 260 ships were loaded and set sail from Sandy Hook, New Jersey. The most direct approach by sea to Philadelphia was to sail out into the Atlantic Ocean and sail south to the Delaware Bay. Ships could navigate up the Delaware River and land below the city. Howe was reluctant to navigate the Delaware because rumors had reached him of American built river defenses. Instead the British sailed up the Chesapeake, approaching the city from the southwest.

In the meantime, Washington moved his Army to the Delaware, stopping on the New Jersey side of Coryell's Ferry, the site of present day Lambertville, to wait for reports confirming the location of the British troops. On August 22nd Howe's ships were reported in the Chesapeake. Washington, certain that Philadelphia was the target, prepared to defend the city.

ELFRETH'S ALLEY

Philadelphia, Pennsylvania

On August 24th Washington and his army marched through Philadelphia in a show of strength to restore confidence and boost the morale of Congress and the citizens as the British moved closer to the city. From his camp near Germantown, Washington prepared his 15,000 troops for the display. Washington and the Marquis de LaFayette led the army down Front Street and up Chestnut Street to the sound of fifes and drums.

The residents of Elfreth's Alley surely heard the fifes and drums and gathered at the end of their street to see the army march past. This block of houses, many of which were built before the American Revolution, remains to this day as a reminder of middle class life during the Revolution. As part of the commercial center of Philadelphia, it provided living and working space for craftspeople and shopkeepers of the city.

Elfreth's Alley Association, Inc.

126 Elfreth's Alley • Philadelphia, PA 19106 • 215-574-0560

Elfreth's Alley was created between 1702 and 1704 and is known as the oldest residential street in the nation. The thirty houses lining the Alley today were built between 1728 and 1836 and were occupied by middle class craftspeople and shopkeepers. Elfreth's Alley and its neighborhood, the Old City section of Philadelphia, was the commercial center of the city during the 1700's. The marketplace and first City Hall were located two blocks south of the Alley at Second and Market Streets, and the waterfront wharves were located just east of the Alley beyond the present site of I-95. Alley houses reflect a variety of architectural styles found during the 18th century. Number 120 and 122 (built 1728), reflect early smaller houses, while Number 121 (built 1800) reflects larger and later Federal style houses. During Colonial times the word alley had a very different meaning than it does today. Then, an alley was a quiet residential street, not an access way for service and commercial traffic.

All of these houses are privately owned. Visitors are invited to tour during the Alley's Open House held the first Sunday in June and during the Annual Christmas Tours in December. Number 126, "The Mantua Makers' House," is operated as a museum, and is open to the public.

In 1963, the United States Department of the Interior, National Park Service, recognized the significance of Elfreth's Alley and designated it a National Historic Landmark.

RESOURCES
Oldest residential street in Philadelphia & the nation; open house first Sunday in June & Christmas tours in December. Call for information.

MUSEUM
No. 126 has been restored & furnished to its 18th century appearance; interpretive exhibit; museum shop; courtyard garden.

EDUCATION PROGRAMS
Outreach program available on request.

EDUCATION MATERIALS
An excellent guide book to Elfreth's Alley is available from the Association.

TOUR INFORMATION
Groups are escorted through the museum on a ten minute tour. Guided tours are limited to thirty per group. Advance reservations requested for group tours. Self-guided tours of the house and the block are available for individuals. While touring, note the varied architecture, as well as the fire marks and busybody mirrors. These mirrors, mounted next to the second floor windows, were used to discretely view visitors at the door. Call for information and reservations.

ADMISSION
Free

HOURS
Daily, 10:00 a.m. to 4:00 p.m. Weekends only in January & February. Closed major holidays.

LOCATION & PARKING
Off Second between Arch & Race Streets, Old City section of Philadelphia. Parking is not available at the site. Vehicle and bus parking at 125 Second Street between Chestnut & Walnut Streets.

Yankee Doodle

1.
Fath'r and I went down to camp,
Along with Captain Good'-in
And there we saw the men and boys
As thick as has-ty pud-in.'

CHORUS:
Yankee Doodle keep it up,
Yankee Doodle dandy,
Mind the music and the step,
And with the girls be handy.

2.
And there we see a thousand men,
As rich as Squire David;
And what they wasted ev'ry day,
I wish it could be saved.

CHORUS

3.
And there was Captain Washington
Upon a slapping stallion
A giving orders to his men;
I guess there was a million.

CHORUS

4.
And then the feathers on his hat
They looked so very fine, ah!
I wanted peskily to get
To give to my Jemima.

CHORUS

Instructions

Yankee Doodle was originally written by the British to poke fun at the "Yankee" troops who aided them in the French & Indian War. The song was adopted by the Americans during the Revolutionary War, and it was a favorite tune of the soldiers. Many versions of the song have been written over the years. Space is provided for you to write your own version of this popular song.

Yankee Doodle

by

____

______________________ , 19______

1. ____

____

____

____

2. ____

____

____

____

3. ____

____

____

____

4. ____

____

____

____

August 24, 1777, *Head of Elk, MD*
General Howe and army land, prepare to attack Philadelphia.

August 28, 1777, *Head of Elk, MD*
After a rest marked by bad weather, the British are on the move.

September 9, 1777, *Chadds Ford, PA*
Washington begins to position his troops along the Brandywine River.

September 11, 1777

Army Defeated at Brandywine: British Take Philadelphia

After the long summer of 1777 Washington had assembled the largest fighting force the Americans had mustered to date, about 15,000 men fit for duty. For the first time in the war Washington was not extensively outnumbered by the British. Washington's river defenses near Philadelphia on the Delaware River had been enough to discourage the British from sailing into the Delaware, forcing them to take the longer route up the Chesapeake Bay. As the British moved their force by ship towards Philadelphia, Washington prepared to oppose their attempt to capture the American capital. After 33 days at sea, the British landed at Head of Elk, Maryland, present day Elkton, and they began preparations to march on Philadelphia. After some maneuvering Washington placed the American army between Philadelphia and the British on the east side of the Brandywine River at Chadds Ford. Washington positioned his army along the River, believing he had blocked all of the other nearby "fords," the shallow places in the river that could easily be crossed. In position, Washington and his army waited for the British.

On the morning of September 11, 1777 General Howe sent General von Knyphausen with 5,000 British troops to keep Washington occupied at Chadds Ford. Meanwhile, Howe crossed at a ford the Americans were unaware of, and he marched around Washington's right flank with 13,000 men. Howe had used this tactic successfully against Washington at the Battle of Long Island, and it fooled Washington again. When Washington finally became aware that Howe's force had moved, he attempted to oppose it, but he was not in time. After a valiant defense, the Americans were forced to retreat.

BRANDYWINE BATTLEFIELD PARK
Chadds Ford, Pennsylvania

Although the Quakers were opposed to war, it is well known that cordial relations existed between the Quakers living at Brandywine and the Revolutionary effort. Locally, two prominent Quakers opened their homes to General Washington and his aide, General Marquis de LaFayette. On the eve of the battle, Washington established his headquarters in the farmhouse of Benjamin Ring, a prominent farmer and miller. North of the Ring farm stood the farm of Gideon Gilpin, another Quaker. This house

became the quarters of LaFayette. The houses stood within easy access of Chadd's Ford where it was felt the British army would attempt to cross the Brandywine Creek.

Brandywine Battlefield

P.O. Box 202 • Chadds Ford, Pennsylvania 19317 • 215-459-3342

Brandywine Battlefield consists of fifty acres including the headquarters of Generals Washington and LaFayette prior to the Battle of Brandywine. Today's park stands at the rear of the main American lines during the battle. After the retreat of the American forces to Chester, the British thoroughly plundered the two properties. Gideon Gilpin filed a claim for his losses which gives some insight into the appearance of the farm in September 1777. The claim lists losses of: "10 milch cows, 1 yoke of oxen, 48 sheep, 28 swine, 12 tons of hay, 230 bushels of wheat, saddle and bridle, 50 pounds of bacon, a history book, 1 gun, 4,000 (fence) rails, 1 clock," etc. In addition to making a claim for items lost to the British, Gilpin in August 1778 petitioned the court for a license to operate a tavern in his house in order to recover some of his losses.

In July, 1825, LaFayette, on his triumphal tour of America almost fifty years after the battle, stopped at the farm with his son and visited with old Gideon Gilpin who by then was 87 years old and confined to his bed.

After the Revolution, the two houses were owned by various families. LaFayette's quarters was acquired by the Commonwealth of Pennsylvania in 1949 and is now restored to its 1777 appearance. Washington's headquarters gradually fell into ruin and eventually burned. Extensive reconstruction work was done in the 1950's. Today, the house is furnished as it would have been prior to the Battle of Brandywine.

The park and these historic properties are owned and operated by the Pennsylvania Historical and Museum Commission in conjunction with the Brandywine Battlefield Park Commission.

RESOURCES

Restored and furnished historic buildings; 50 acre park; special events.

VISITOR CENTER

Begin the tour at the Visitor Center with an audio-visual program and interpretive exhibition highlighting the Philadelphia Campaign of 1777. Tickets for the historic houses are sold here. Museum shop & book store.

TOUR INFORMATION

Guided group tours of the site, including the historic houses, are available with advance reservations. Guides provide interpretation of the historic houses for the visitors. Brochures and interpretive literature are available at the Visitor Center. Call for reservations.

FOOD SERVICE

Picnic area available.

ADMISSION

Adults $ 1.00; seniors $ .75; children $ .50; organized school groups free.

HOURS

Tuesday—Saturday, 9:00 a.m. to 5:00 p.m. Sunday, Noon to 5:00 p.m.

LOCATION & PARKING

On Route 1 west of Route 202, Chadds Ford, PA. Vehicle and bus parking on park grounds.

General Marquis de LaFayette

Reconnaissance Map

BATTLE
OF
BRANDYWINE
in which
THE REBELS
were defeated,
September the 11th 1777,
by the Army under the Command of
GENERAL S.r WILL.m HOWE.

Both armies employed map makers to survey and draw maps of the terrain. If the maps were accurate, they aided the commanders in making a battle plan. If they were not accurate, they could lead to confusion and even defeat. Washington's defeat at Brandywine was caused in part because his maps were inaccurate. On the day of the Battle, Washington and his officers were confused about the location of the British forces. This allowed the British to mount a surprise attack against the Americans. With a good map of the Brandywine area which marked the location and names of all fords, Washington would have been prepared for the attack by the British.

Instructions

On the following page draw a reconnaissance map of your neighborhood. Start by determining what direction north is from your house. If you don't know what direction north is, remember that the sun rises in the east and sets in the west. Next, begin drawing in the roads and streets. Include their names. Then, add all of the buildings in the neighborhood including houses, apartment buildings, stores, and gas stations. Next, add any significant features of the landscape. Include natural features, such as hills, forests, and large trees, and man made features, such as billboards, traffic signals, and fire hydrants. You might want to develop symbols for the various types of buildings and features you will include in your map. An x might be used to mark the location of all houses, while an o might mark the site of all fire hydrants. Finally, complete the key to your map by drawing all symbols used and indicating their meaning in the box provided.

Develop a plan to defend your neighborhood against a British attack from the north.

Reconnaissance Map of My Neighborhood

KEY

September 18, 1777, *Valley Forge, PA*
British capture American food and supplies stored at Valley Forge.

September 19, 1777, *Philadelphia, PA*
Congress abandons Philadelphia; reconvenes in Lancaster, PA.

September 21, 1777, *Paoli, PA*
British attack Gen. Wayne's men; American's suffer heavy losses.

September 18 - 26, 1777

American Army at Pottsgrove Supplies Secured in Reading

After the defeat at Brandywine, the American army was forced to retreat. During the next several days, General Howe and his Army moved closer to Philadelphia with little opposition from Washington. Congress moved from Philadelphia to Lancaster and then to York, relocating important military stores from Philadelphia to Reading, Pennsylvania in anticipation of the British takeover of Philadelphia.

On September 18th, Washington's army set up camp near Pottsgrove, Pennsylvania. The camp was located on the outskirts of the little village of Pottsgrove, in a triangular area north of the Great Road (what is now Route 422) and on both sides of the Swamp Pike. From that position the Americans could block the main roads to Reading, protecting the American supplies located there. The army could also get the rest they needed, wait for reinforcements, and try to restore their morale before moving against the British. Washington's force had dropped to 6,000 from a high of nearly 15,000 only a few weeks before. Washington wrote to Alexander Hamilton on the 22nd, "The distressed situation of the army, for want of blankets and many necessary articles of clothing, is truly deplorable, and inevitably must bring destruction to it, unless a speedy remedy is applied."

The defeat at Brandywine and the subsequent movements of Washington to protect his position allowed the British to take Philadelphia without a battle. On September 26th Cornwallis and the British army marched into Philadelphia. Howe established an outpost at Germantown.

POTTSGROVE MANSION
Pottstown, Pennsylvania

Ironmaster Thomas Potts, eldest son of John Potts (d. 1768), was the owner of Pottsgrove Mansion during the Fall of 1777 while the Continental Army camped in the surrounding area. Thomas Potts was commissioned a Colonel in Washington's army. It is thought that during the stay at Pottsgrove, Washington visited Thomas at the mansion and enjoyed his hospitality there. Potts and other local leaders did what they could to supply the army with meat, bread, potatoes, shoes, and clothing. Reinforcements sent by Congress began to arrive, and by September 25th Washington felt the army

was sufficiently ready to move again. On September 26th the Army marched out of Camp Pottsgrove determined to force the British out of Philadelphia.

Pottsgrove Mansion

West King Street • Pottstown, Pennsylvania 19464 • 215-326-4014

Pottsgrove Mansion sits on a high hill overlooking the Great Road and the Schuylkill River. Colonel Potts' father, John, built the house in the early 1750's after acquiring his fortune in the iron industry. He had it constructed in the English fashion, called the Georgian style after King George, with a large central hallway, grand staircase, carved and paneled woodwork, and high ceilings. Such a large house had to be sturdy, so local sandstone blocks were used to build walls two feet thick. He followed a building custom of the local Pennsylvania German people by putting on a pent roof and pent eaves. When John Potts was alive, he filled the house with fine furniture, china, and silver. During the army's short encampment at Pottsgrove, it was undoubtedly one of the finest residences in the area.

Many of the Potts children served the American cause in the War for Independence. Thomas served as a Colonel in the Continental army. Samuel, the second son, engaged with the Committee of Safety in March of 1776 to cast "a number of cannons for the use of the Province" at Warwick Furnace, an ironworks in which his father had given him a share. He was also a member of the State Constitutional Convention. Jonathon Potts did not follow into the iron business, but became a physician instead. He was a member of the first graduating class of the Pennsylvania Academy (later University of Pennsylvania). When war came, Congress appointed him Deputy Director General of Hospitals for the Northern Department of the Army, and later for the Middle Department. Isaac Potts, the fourth son, owned the house used as Washington's headquarters during the Valley Forge winter.

Today, Pottsgrove Mansion is owned and operated by the Pennsylvania Historical and Museum Commission with support from the Pottstown Historical Society. The house, restored to its 18th century splendor, features outstanding examples of period furniture and decorative arts.

RESOURCES

Restored and furnished 18th century home; research library; museum shop & bookstore; special events.

EDUCATIONAL PROGRAMS

Colonial craft workshops are offered for the general public. Call for information.

TOUR INFORMATION

A staff member or volunteer escorts groups or individuals through the Pottsgrove Mansion on a 30 minute tour. Advance reservations required for group tours. Self-guided tours of the house are not available. Call for reservations.

LIBRARY

The Pottstown Historical Society maintains a research library in the Pottsgrove Mansion. Their holdings include genealogical records, manuscripts, and books on local history, decorative arts, and the American Revolution. The library is open by appointment only. Call for information.

FOOD SERVICE

Picnicking is allowed on the grounds.

ADMISSION

Adults $ 1.50; seniors $ 1.00; students (ages 6-17) $ .50; organized school groups free; adult groups $ 1.00.

HOURS

Wednesday—Saturday, 9:00 a.m. to 5:00 p.m. Sunday, Noon to 5:00 p.m. Closed state holidays (except Memorial Day, Independence Day & Labor Day).

LOCATION & PARKING

Route 100 & King St., Pottstown, PA. Vehicle and bus parking on site grounds.

October 2 - 4, 1777

Washington Plans Offensive Against Enemy In Philadelphia

Washington and his men were humiliated by their inability to protect Philadelphia from the British force. The Americans were outmaneuvered during the days following their defeat at Brandywine, allowing the British to march into Philadelphia unopposed on September 26th. That same day Washington and his army marched from Pottsgrove to Pennypacker's Mill along the Perkiomen Creek just outside present day Schwenksville, Pennsylvania. Reinforcements continued to arrive, and Washington estimated to Congress on September 28th that he had 8,000 Continental soldiers and 3,000 militia fit for duty at Pennypacker's Mill. A council of war considered an attack on the British in Germantown, but the generals voted ten to five against an attack at this time. Instead, the army moved closer to Philadelphia to observe the enemy force.

On October 2, the Continental army set up camp at Center Point only fifteen miles from Germantown. Washington selected the stylish home of Peter Wentz for his headquarters. A council of war was again called, and Washington found that circumstances had changed to his favor. The British had deployed a large number of troops to escort supplies to Philadelphia, capture the Delaware River fort at Billingsport, and reinforce the troops in Philadelphia itself, leaving only 9,000 men at Germantown. Washington and his Generals decided the time was right for an attack. During the next few days at the Peter Wentz Farmstead, Washington planned the tactics and strategies for his attack of the British force at Germantown, confident of victory.

PETER WENTZ FARMSTEAD

Montgomery County, Pennsylvania

In 1777 the Peter Wentz farmstead covered approximately 300 acres of rolling farmland along the Skippack Road. Its convenient location and stylish comfort led Washington to select the farmstead for his headquarters both before and after the Battle of Germantown. It was at Wentz farmstead that Washington finalized the plans for the battle. During each of his visits to the farmstead, Washington was given the two upstairs, front rooms for his office and bedroom, and the winter kitchen for his cook's use to prepare meals. Local tradition tells us that the fear of poisoning was so strong that the cook stayed in the kitchen day and night, leaving it only when absolutely necessary. While a few of the General's

closest aides might have been quartered at the Wentz house, probably Peter and Rosanna Wentz retained a portion of the house for their own use.

Peter Wentz Farmstead

P.O. Box 240 • Worcester, Pennsylvania 19490 • 215-584-5104

Peter Wentz Jr., anticipating his inheritance by several years, began in 1744 to improve the property that would eventually become his. In that year he built a stone barn and a log dwelling. In 1758 a fashionable, substantial stone house was added, and the log structure was relegated to other uses. Peter Wentz sold the farmstead during the economic depression of 1784 and moved to a smaller house about three miles east on the Skippack Road. The new owner, a land speculator named Van Bieber, held the property for ten years, then sold it to Melchior Schultz, a minister in the Schwenkfelder church. The Farmstead remained in the Schultz family until 1969, when it was purchased by the Commissioners of Montgomery County. Restoration to its 1777 configuration was begun in 1971 and the Farmstead opened to the public in 1976. Reconstruction of the drastically altered 1744 barn was begun in 1977 and completed in 1980. Additional outbuildings and dependencies are still being reconstructed as archaeological investigation proves their 1777 existence.

The Peter Wentz Farmstead reflects Wentz's German background. Although the house follows the Georgian style of architecture, popular with the wealthy English gentry in the area, many German characteristics are used. Such features are the paling (a form of insulation in the ceiling of the cellar), the exposed floor joists in the rear portion of the house, the five-plate stoves that heat the dining room and bedroom, the brightly colored woodwork with brush and sponge decoration on the walls and dadoes, and the decorative hardware found on the doors.

Today, the Farmstead is presented as a working farm of the 18th century, featuring livestock, an orchard planted with early apple varieties, fields of flax, and a kitchen garden.

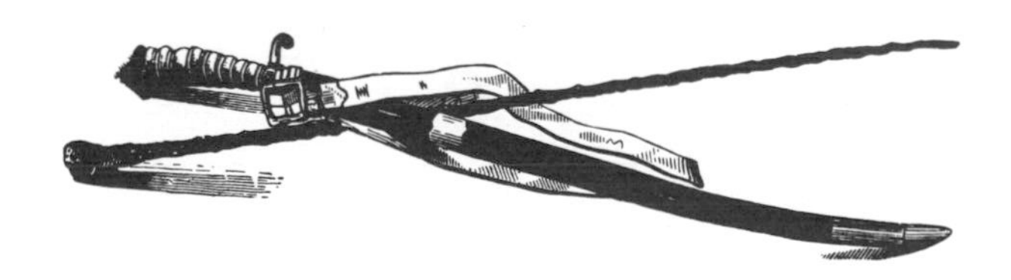

RESOURCES
18th Century farmstead: restored & furnished house; restored barnyard; orchard; kitchen garden; fields; special events.

VISITOR CENTER
The Reception Center features an audio-visual program, gift shop, & bookstore.

EDUCATIONAL PROGRAMS
A highlight of the farmstead is its on-going 18th Century Craft Program. Authentic demonstrations of Colonial crafts are presented on Saturday afternoons. With a minimum of 4 week's notice, special demonstrations are available for school groups visiting the farmstead or in their classroom before or after their visit. Demonstrations may also be scheduled for area senior centers. Call for information and reservations.

EDUCATIONAL MATERIALS
A pre-tour packet of educational materials is available to school groups free of charge. The audio-visual orientation program is available for classroom use.

TOUR INFORMATION
Tours begin in the Reception Center with an audio-visual orientation program. Costumed volunteer guides escort visitors through the house. The tour emphasizes the American Revolution, farm life, architecture, and Pennsylvania German traditions. Tours of the barnyard are available by special request. Self-guided tours are not available. Groups of ten or more must have a reservation. The last scheduled tour for the general public is 3:30 p.m. Call for reservations.

LIBRARY
The farmstead houses a small research library featuring books on local history and the Revolutionary War. Open by appointment only. Call for reservations.

FOOD SERVICE
Picnicking is allowed on the grounds.

ADMISSION
Free

HOURS
Tuesday—Saturday, 10 a.m. to 4 p.m. Sunday 1 p.m. to 4 p.m. Closed the second week of September, Thanksgiving, Christmas, and New Years's Day.

LOCATION & PARKING
On Route 73, Worcester Township, at Schultz Road, in Montgomery County. Vehicle and bus parking on the site grounds.

October 4, 1777

American Army Defeated At Germantown

British General William Howe recognized the strategic importance of Germantown as soon as his troops captured the city of Philadelphia in late September, 1777. Protected by the Schuylkill River on one side and the Delaware River on the other, Philadelphia was situated on a peninsula. Any American attack would come by land, most likely through Germantown.

Washington's plan, conceived at the Peter Wentz farmstead, called for the simultaneous advance of four different units of troops. At dawn, the four columns were to converge at Market Square in Germantown, not far from British General Howe's headquarters.

The quiet community of Germantown was transformed into a battleground during the early morning hours of October 4th when Washington's troops attacked the British stronghold there. Washington's plan went astray when one of his four columns lost its bearings. Others failed to coordinate effectively. Fog and gunsmoke made it hard to tell friend from foe. The defense was particularly strong at Cliveden, and valuable time was lost while the Americans attacked the house. Bad luck and poor timing forced Washington to retreat to Whitemarsh with the British in pursuit.

The battle was an American defeat, but it served to boost the troop's morale and self confidence for they believed they had almost won the battle. They believed their defeat was the result of bad luck, not poor tactics.

CLIVEDEN

Philadelphia, Pennsylvania

Throughout the advance, Washington's troops found themselves facing enemy fire. The defense was particularly strong at a large stone house on Germantown Avenue—Benjamin Chew's summer home, Cliveden. Inside the house about 120 members of the British Fortieth of Foot, an infantry unit under the command of Lt. Col. Thomas Musgrave, fired muskets from the upstairs windows. Reports claim that Henry Knox, head of Washington's artillery, convinced the General that Cliveden should not go unattacked, so Washington ordered cannon to fire upon the house.

Cliveden, built of local graystone two feet thick, was like a fortress. Muskets and field cannon were ineffective against its walls. An attempt to set fire to the house failed. More than fifty men of American General William Maxwell's brigade died trying to breach Cliveden's walls.

Cliveden

6401 Germantown Avenue • Philadelphia, PA 19144 • 215-848-1777

Cliveden, the summer home of Benjamin Chew, a famous lawyer and jurist, took local stonemasons and wood-carvers four years to build between 1763 and 1767. Benjamin Chew, his wife, thirteen daughters, and one son spent summers in Germantown to escape the hot, smelly, city.

As a man of wealth and position, Benjamin Chew and his family had many important friends, including the Logans and the Shippens. John Adams and Thomas Jefferson visited the Chews in their town house, and they may have visited Cliveden, as well. LaFayette, on his return to the United States in 1825, visited Cliveden for a grand reception.

Several years after the Battle of Germantown, Benjamin Chew sold Cliveden, in part because he was disappointed with the damage caused there during the battle. But, he liked the house enough to buy it back seventeen years later. After that, Cliveden continued as a Chew family residence for nearly two hundred years. Through the generosity of Benjamin Chew's descendants, the mansion was acquired by the National Trust for Historic Preservation in June 1972.

Cliveden is richly furnished with Philadelphia Chippendale and federal style furniture, some of which was purchased from Governor John Penn. Many pieces are attributed to Philadelphia's most famous furniture craftsmen, such as Thomas Affleck, Jonathan Gostelowe, Joseph Reynolds, and David Evans. Original fabrics, clothing, and Chew's law library also survive in their original setting. The Chew family papers, estimated at more than 100,000 manuscript pages covering two centuries of family life, reveal much about Cliveden's past and its historic relationship to early Philadelphia and the nation.

RESOURCES
Restored and furnished 18th century house; special events; preservation programs; gardens.

VISITOR CENTER
The interior of the carriage house has been converted into a contemporary visitors' facility featuring a museum shop & bookstore, exhibit area, and lunch facility which is available by appointment only.

EDUCATIONAL MATERIALS
Educational materials to supplement school group visits are being prepared on the "Battle of Germantown" and "Life in Germantown During the 18th Century." Please call for information.

TOUR INFORMATION
Volunteers escort individuals and groups through the house on a 35 minute tour. The tour emphasizes the life of Benjamin Chew and his family, the American Revolution including the Battle of Germantown, architecture, and decorative arts. Self-guided tours are not available. Tours for the general public are conducted on the hour from 10 a.m. to 3 p.m. Call for group reservations.

FOOD SERVICE
Lunch is available to groups with prior arrangements. A bag lunchroom can be reserved for school groups with prior arrangements. Call at least four weeks before your scheduled visit.

ADMISSION
Adults $ 2.00; seniors $ 1.50; children $ 1.00.

HOURS
Open from April 1st to December 31st; Tuesday through Saturday, 10:00 a.m. to 4:00 p.m., Sunday, 1:00 p.m. to 4:00 p.m. Closed Easter, Thanksgiving & Christmas.

LOCATION & PARKING
6401 Germantown Avenue north of Johnson Street, entrance off Cliveden Street. Street parking along Cliveden St. is available for cars and buses.

Additional Germantown Sites

DESHLER-MORRIS HOUSE

The National Park Service
5442 Germantown Avenue
Philadelphia, PA 19144
215-596-1748

In 1793 and 1794, when yellow fever epidemics forced the Federal Government out of Philadelphia, George Washington and his family moved to the Deshler-Morris House.

GERMANTOWN MENNONITE INFORMATION CENTER & JOHNSON HOUSE

6117 Germantown Avenue
Philadelphia, PA 19144
215-843-0943

The Johnson house was built in 1768 by John Johnson a Quaker. During the Battle of Germantown, fighting occured around the house. A fence and stone wall became a breastwork during the battle.

GRUMBLETHORPE

5267 Germantown Avenue
Philadelphia, PA 19144
215-843-4820
or 215-925-2251

Grumblethorpe, built in 1744 by Philadelphia merchant, John Wister, served as headquarters for British officers during the Battle of Germantown.

STENTON MANSION

18th & Windrim Streets
Philadelphia, PA 19140
215-329-7312

Stenton, the country home of James Logan, housed Washington on August 23rd, 1777. The house was the headquarters of General Sir William Howe during the Battle of Germatown.

Call for information about hours and admission at these sites.

American Attack on the Chew House Battle of Germantown

Washington's Uncertainty after the Battle of Germantown

Head Quarters 19th Octr., 1777

Dr. Sir,

I have receiv'd your Letter by the bearer and am exceeding sorry to find your Brigade so much weaken'd — what can be the meaning of it? — I have no doubt but that you will render all the Service you can with those you have, & therefore shall say nothing more on that head — The Enemy have totally abandoned German Town — I sent a large Detachment there this Morning who got down just as they had withdrawn their Picquets. — the whole Army will move downwards at four Oclock in the Morning when we shall be nearer to you. —

I am not so much of opinion that the Enemy are about to remove from Phila. as that they are meditating a serious attack upon our defence of the River — for this reason it is that I wish you could annoy them that way if possible.

I am Dr. Sir
yr. Most Obedt. St.
Go. Washington

PS. Is there no getting more of the Militia of Chester etca. to your aid?

A letter from George Washington to General Potter.

November 2 -December 11, 1777

Americans at Whitemarsh

After the Battle of Germantown, Washington was forced to retreat with the British force in pursuit. During the next several weeks, Washington and his Army moved from place to place through what is today Montgomery County, Pennsylvania. The army marched, set up camp, broke camp, and marched again, setting up camps at Pennypacker's Mill, Kulpsville, Peter Wentz Farmstead, Whitpain Township, and finally arriving in Whitemarsh on November 2nd.

From Whitemarsh, only a few miles from Philadelphia, Washington hoped to launch another attack on the British force holding the city. On October 19th Howe concentrated his troops in the heart of Philadelphia, withdrawing the force at Germantown. At a council of war held on November 25th, Washington and his Generals debated their course of action. A few felt that an attack on the British force in the Philadelphia area could only lead to victory, but the majority believed this was an impossible move to make — one that certainly would end in defeat.

While the army camped at Whitemarsh and debated a course of action, Howe marched out of Philadelphia on December 4th with most of his force to attempt a surprise attack on the Whitemarsh encampment. News of this reached Washington, and he reinforced the Whitemarsh encampment in anticipation of the battle. After several minor engagements Howe and his army returned to Philadelphia. Howe refused to risk his army in an all out attack on the Whitemarsh defenses.

FORT WASHINGTON STATE PARK

Fort Washington, Pennsylvania

Fort Washington State Park and the community of Fort Washington, take their name from the Fort built here by American Revolutionary soldiers in the fall of 1777. Whitemarsh, as the area was called then, provided a defendable encampment site for Washington and 12,000 soldiers from November 2nd until December 11th, 1777. From the hills of Whitemarsh, Washington could keep an eye on the British force in Philadelphia and mount an attack if the opportunity arose. Earthen fortifications were constructed on the three nearby hills—Fort Hill, Militia Hill, and Camp Hill—in an effort to make the area more secure.

HOPE LODGE & MATHER MILL

Fort Washington, Pennsylvania

Hope Lodge, then the home of William West, served as the headquarters of Dr. John Cochran and the Army Medical Department during the Army's encampment at Whitemarsh. Makeshift hospitals located throughout the camp served the many sick and wounded. Dr. Cochran and his surgeons deplored the wretched conditions under which they were forced to treat the soldiers. Filth and overcrowding along with shortages of medical supplies, clothing, sheets, and blankets made their jobs all but impossible. Six desperately needed doctors died of fever which raged throughout the camp. The sick and wounded were eventually moved to Easton, Bethlehem, Allentown, and Reading as the main army moved to Valley Forge.

Fort Washington State Park
Department of Environmental Resources

500 Bethlehem Pike • Fort Washington, PA 19034 • 215-646-2942

Fort Washington State Park consists of 493 acres in eastern Montgomery County. The park is primarily a recreational facility, offering visitors the opportunity to hike, sled, or cross-country ski on the park's wooded slopes and open fields where Washington's army camped in 1777. The park is divided into four geographic areas—Fort Hill, Militia Hill, Sandy Run, and Flourtown. Fort Hill was the western end of the Continental troop positions, and it was the site of the fort structure which gives the park its name. All traces of the fort have disappeared, but during the 1930's, a reconstruction of the earth redoubt was built following the lines of the original fort as closely as possible. The Pennsylvania Militia, under the command of Generals Armstrong, Cadwalader, and Irvine, had their positions along the ridge of Militia Hill.

Although Fort Washington is beyond the boundaries of Philadelphia, the city's Fairmount Park Commission began acquiring land there in the early 1920's. The Fairmount Park Commission along with the Secretary of the Commonwealth's Department of Forests and Waters administered the park until 1953. In that year, an Act by the State Legislature turned the park over to the former Department of Forests and Waters, now the Department of Environmental Resources.

RESOURCES
Historic Site; recreational park; nature area; hiking trails; group camping facility; picnic pavilions; special events.

EDUCATIONAL PROGRAMS
The park offers an orientation program to the site and its history for groups with advance reservations. Nature walks and special programs are offered from April to Labor Day. Call for information and reservations.

TOUR INFORMATION
Groups and individuals tour the park on a self-guided basis. Interpretive literature and maps are available at the park office.

LIBRARY
The Historical Society of Fort Washington maintains The E. Hamilton Parke research library at the Clifton House. The library features historical society publications, rare books, Pennsylvania archives, county histories, Civil War records, biographies, and genealogies.

FOOD SERVICE
A mobile food vendor makes regular rounds throughout the picnic areas from Memorial Day to Labor Day.

ADMISSION
Free

HOURS
Daily, 8:00 a.m. to Sunset

LOCATION & PARKING
Bethlehem Pike, off exit 26 of PA Turnpike. Vehicle and bus parking available in park.

ADDITIONAL SITES
The historic **Clifton House** is operated by the Fort Washington Historical Society as a local history museum. Call or write for tour and program information:

Clifton House
473 Bethlehem Pike
Fort Washington, PA 19034
215-646-6065

Medicine During the Revolution

The medical practices and procedures used during the American Revolution might be considered primitive or even barbaric by today's standards. Little accurate information about disease, sanitation, or even biology was known at that time. A soldier was far more likely to die under medical supervision than on the battlefield.

In an attempt to maintain a healthy army, the Continental Congress established a Hospital Department at the beginning of the war. Congress' good intentions had little benefit for the soldier in the field. Lack of funds, bureaucratic mismanagement, and shortages of drugs, equipment, and supplies hampered the efforts of the Hospital Department.

Hospitals became a breeding ground for disease. Men were stuffed into every available space. The men rested on straw spread on the floor right next to one another so disease spread quickly from one man to the next. Typhoid, smallpox, yellow fever, as well as measles, dysentery, and lice were a constant threat. Bloodletting — cutting into a vein and drawing as much as 10 to 12 ounces of blood each day —and blistering — applying a caustic solution to the skin to raise a blister — were common treatments during the period. Both had serious consequences. One step towards modern medicine was taken during this time, however. Washington had his troops inoculated against smallpox during the Morristown encampment of 1777.

Diderot's *Encyclopdia*
18th Century Apothecary—Surgeons Tools.

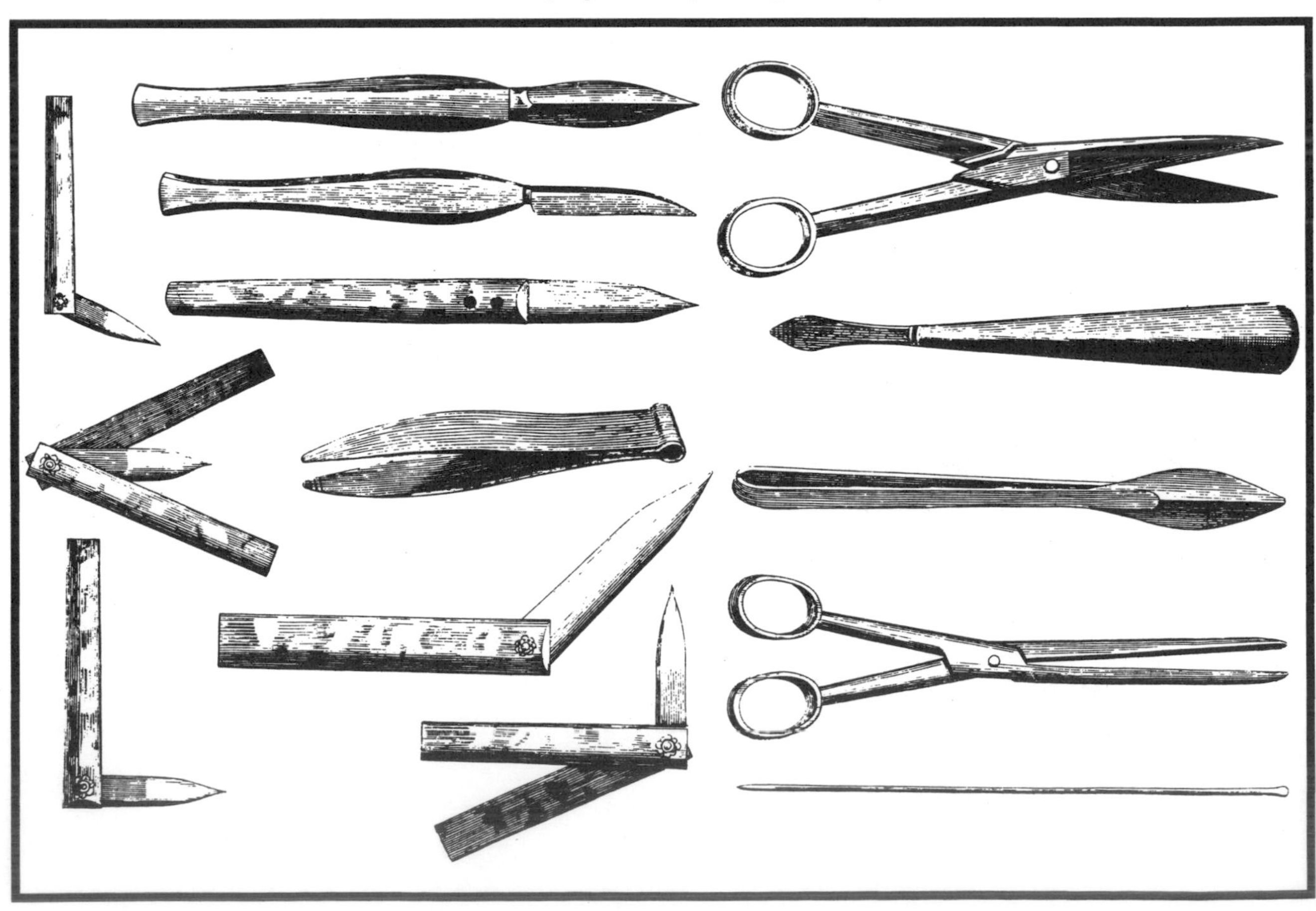

Hope Lodge & Mather Mill

553 Bethlehem Pike • Fort Washington, PA 19034 • 215-646-1595

Hope Lodge, built 1743-1748 by Samuel Morris, a Quaker entrepreneur, was the grandest house in the Whitemarsh Valley at the time of the 1777 encampment. Built in the English Georgian style, the house is one of the most outstanding examples of pre-revolutionary architecture in America.

The house was purchased in 1776 by William West, a wealthy Philadelphia businessman and ardent supporter of the Continental Congress and its rebel army. West purchased the Whitemarsh estate out of fear that the British would soon invade Philadelphia. If his hope was to avoid the entanglements of war, the events of the late Fall of 1777 would prove that he had not moved quite far enough from the city.

Mather Mill, an 1830 gristmill, was built on land once owned by the original owner of Hope Lodge, Samuel Morris. The mill is located across Bethlehem Pike from Hope Lodge and today serves the local community as a meeting room, lecture hall and special events facility.

RESOURCES

Restored and furnished 18th century house; herb and flower gardens; special events.

EDUCATIONAL PROGRAMS

Special educational programs are available to school groups with advance reservations.

TOUR INFORMATION

A staff member escorts groups or individuals through Hope Lodge on a one hour tour. Tours can be tailored to the interests of the group, emphasizing architecture, decorative arts, or family life. Advance reservations required for group tours. Self-guided tours of the house are not available.

FOOD SERVICE

Picnicking is allowed on the grounds.

ADMISSION

Adults $ 1.50; seniors $ 1.00; children $ .50; organized school groups free.

HOURS

Tuesday—Saturday, 9:00 a.m. to 5:00 p.m.
Sunday, Noon to 5:00 p.m.

LOCATION & PARKING

553 Bethlehem Pike, off exit 26 of PA Turnpike. Vehicle and bus parking on site grounds.

September & October 1777

Delaware River Defenses Reinforced and Manned

At the start of the Revolution, Congress realized the importance of securing Philadelphia against a sea attack and ordered the construction of numerous river defense systems. The Pennsylvania Council of Safety oversaw the planning and construction of these fortifications. Their plan, developed in July 1775, called for the construction of land batteries along the Pennsylvania and New Jersey shores of the Delaware River, the organization of a navy to guard the river, and the construction of underwater obstructions to be placed along the river bottom.

Three sites were selected for the land batteries. Mud Island on the Pennsylvania side of the Delaware was the site of Fort Mifflin. Directly opposite Mud Island was Red Bank, the site of Fort Mercer. Four miles downstream from Red Bank a fortification was constructed at Billingsport, New Jersey. Several engineers developed designs for the defenses, but the designs proved to be too ambitious to complete entirely before the British threatened the defenses. As the British moved closer to Philadelphia, the planned fortifications at Billingsport and Fort Mercer were reduced in scope in an effort to complete and man them before a British attack.

Philadelphia shipwrights designed and constructed numerous "row galleys" that would become the backbone of the newly formed Pennsylvania Navy. These fifty foot boats with a cannon mounted in the bow patrolled the river, attacked British ships sailing up the Delaware, and aided in the city's defense.

CHEVAUX-DE-FRISE
Placed Along Delaware

Congress charged Robert Smith, a Philadelphia architect and carpenter, with the task of blocking the Delaware River against British ships. A system of ***chevaux-de-frise*** was developed. These consisted of a series of iron spikes supported just below the level of the water set so as to impale or impede ships sailing upstream. The iron spikes were mounted on heavy timbers that were mounted at an angle on large wooden boxes. The boxes could be floated into position in the Delaware and then filled with twenty to forty tons of stone to sink and anchor them in place. Each box supported two or three points, and each set of points had to be especially designed for the depth where it would be placed. The ***chevaux-de-frise*** were placed strategically along and across the river, and a few river pilots were given their location so they could safely guide the American vessels in the river.

River Defense Game

A game for two players.

THE PLAYERS:

One player represents the Pennsylvania **COUNCIL OF SAFETY**. The Council of Safety will mark the location of the *chevaux-de-frise* on a secret map (drawn on graph paper). The Council can place 20 *chevaux-de-frise* in the channel to block the British, and at least two safe passages must be left so American ships might pass through. Ships only sail straight or to the side; they do not sail diagonally.

The other player is the CAPTAIN of a British frigate with orders to sail to Philadelphia. The captain can start the perilous trip by sailing into any square in the ZONE OF DEFENSE. The frigate can move quickly enough to avoid enemy bombardments from Forts Mercer and Mifflin as long as it does not run into a *chevaux-de-frise.* When it gets caught on a *chevaux-de-frise*, it must turn back, but each time it does so, the Americans score a hit. The frigate is only strong enough to withstand ten hits.

HOW TO PLAY:

The Council marks off a square on a piece of graph paper 8 squares across and 8 squares down. Label them 1-8 and A-H to match the playing board. Mark the secret location of 20 *chevaux-de-frise* with X's on the graph paper. The Council must leave at least two channels open to Philadelphia.

When the Council has completed the secret map, the frigate can try sailing up river. The captain sails the ship into a square in the first line of the Zone of Defense (in row H) and calls out its name (for example,"H-4"). The Council checks the secret map, and if the space does not have a *chevaux-de-frise*, the Council says "ALL CLEAR". If the square does have a *chevaux-de-frise*, the Council says "DEFENDED." If the square is clear, the captain can sail on. Otherwise, he must mark the square with a token to indicate that he was stopped and a hit was scored, and the frigate must return to the last square it was in. The frigate is not allowed to move diagonally on the board.

Play continues with the frigate continuing to sail up river until it reaches Philadelphia or uses up all ten tokens.

When the game is over, the Council must show the captain the secret map so the captain can see where the safe passages were. The players can take turns defending or sailing, and they can keep score by awarding the captain one point for each token left if the frigate reaches Philadelphia and the Council three points if it does not.

DELAWARE RIVER

PHILADELPHIA (*Finish*)

	1	2	3	4	5	6	7	8
A								
B								
C								
D				ZONE OF DEFENSE				
E								
F								
G								
H								

BILLINGSPORT (*Start*)

FORT MIFFLIN

FORT MERCER

OBJECT OF THE GAME:

To sail from Billingsport to Philadelphia without being sunk.

YOU WILL NEED:

Pencil, graph paper, 10 tokens to represent *chevaux-de-frise* (jacks or buttons will do), 1 token to represent the ship.

October, 1777, *Delaware River*
Pennsylvania Navy under Hazelwood harasses enemy fleet.

October 2, 1777, *Billingsport, NJ*
British attack Billingsport; defense abandoned.

October 3, 1777, *Delaware River*
British begin to clear *chevaux-de-frise* in river.

October 22, 1777

Delaware River Defenses Bombarded

Although the British occupied the city of Philadelphia after the Battle of Brandywine, they were at a serious disadvantage. The extensive American river defenses prevented ships from bringing desperately needed food and supplies to the British army and the citizens of Philadelphia. Without the needed supplies Howe might be forced to evacuate the city during the winter, exposing his men to an attack by the Americans. In an effort to conserve scarce food supplies, he placed the army on half rations in early November.

Howe mustered all his might against the American river defenses using both sea and land power. His first move was against Billingsport. A British force crossed the Delaware and attacked Billingsport from its land side. The garrison was outnumbered and forced to evacuate by boat for Fort Mifflin on October 2nd. During the next two weeks, the British Navy began clearing the ***chevaux-de-frise*** above Billingsport despite constant harassment by the galleys of the Pennsylvania Navy.

After the Battle of Germantown, Howe consolidated his army in Philadelphia in an effort to clear the river defenses. Howe's next move was a major attack against the garrison at Fort Mercer. A British force of Hessians under Colonel Von Donop was ferried over to Cooper's Ferry (now Camden, NJ) spending the night in Haddonfield. On the morning of October 22nd they marched on Fort Mercer.

RED BANK BATTLEFIELD

National Park, New Jersey

The British force in Haddonfield took extensive measures to prevent word of their upcoming attack from reaching the Americans. In spite of these efforts, Jonas Cattell was able to alert Colonel Christopher Greene, commander of the fort, that a British attack was imminent. Soon after 4:00 p.m. the attack began. The Hessians quickly gained the "old" northern section of the fort, only to find themselves before another 10-foot wall and abatis of sharpened tree trunks and branches. As the disordered Hessians moved forward, the Americans continued their defense, fatally wounding hundreds of men, including Von Donop himself. The following day, the 64-gun British warship Augusta, assigned to aid in the battle, exploded and sank off Red Bank Battlefield under heavy American attack. This important victory significantly delayed the British attempt to clear the river defenses.

Red Bank Battlefield

100 Hessian Ave. • National Park, New Jersey 08063 • 609-853-5120

The historic James and Ann Whitall House is the focal point of Red Bank Battlefield today. The house is a modest brick structure with a stone addition. It is built on a bluff along the river. The brick section was probably completed in 1748. James Whitall was a wealthy farmer and merchant. As the family grew, the house was enlarged to include a bedroom and large kitchen in the stone wing of the house. Eventually, the Whitalls had nine children. The main brick portion of the house, which is open to the public, consists of a large keeping room which was the center for everyday life for the Whitall family. Toward the front of the house, facing the river, there is a small farm office where James Whitall conducted farm business.

In 1777 Fort Mercer was built in the Whitall apple orchard immediately north of the dwelling. A portion of the house was commandeered as military quarters. During the attack at Fort Mercer, Ann Whitall refused to abandon her home. The other members of this Quaker family fled to Woodbury. Legend has it that Ann calmly picked up her spinning wheel and went down to the cellar and continued her spinning after a cannonball broke through the north wall of the house. The house was essentially left intact after the battle, and was used as a hospital to care for the wounded.

About 1872, the property was taken over by the United State Government. In 1905 it was transferred to the Gloucester County authority by President Theodore Roosevelt. Today, Red Bank Battlefield is a 26 acre recreational park on the Delaware River commemorating the historic battle of 1777. Portions of the original earthworks have been preserved and reconstructed. Numerous monuments, exhibits, and signs aid visitors in understanding the history of the site. The park is currently undergoing an extensive remodelling and expansion program which will include the restoration of the Whitall House.

RESOURCES
Restored and furnished 18th century house; earthwork fortifications; remnants of *chevaux-de-frise*; recreational facilities; special events.

EDUCATIONAL MATERIALS
Educational brochures featuring the history of the site are available upon request prior to your tour.

TOUR INFORMATION
An interpretive guide escorts groups and individuals on a one hour tour of the Whitall House. Group tours include the grounds and highlight the fortifications and the battle. Self-guided tours of the house are not available. Call for reservations.

LIBRARY
The Gloucester County Historical Society maintains a research library at 17 Hunter Street, Woodbury, NJ. Call 609-845-4771 for information.

FOOD SERVICE
Picnic area available. Call for information.

ADMISSION
Free

HOURS
Daily, May 1st to Labor Day. Weekends only the remainder of the year, 9:00 a.m. to 5:00 p.m.

LOCATION & PARKING
South of Camden on the Delaware River in the city of National Park, NJ. Vehicle and bus parking available on park grounds.

ADDITIONAL SITES
Gloucester County Historical Society Museum
58 N. Broad Street
Woodbury, New Jersey 08096
609-845-4771
Call for information and reservations.

November 15, 1777

Army Evacuates Fort Mifflin: River Defenses Doomed

After the futile attempt to take Fort Mercer on October 22nd the British marshalled all of their available resources against Fort Mifflin in a effort to clear the Delaware River. Fort Mifflin was located on an island and was unprotected from land attack from the northwest. The British used this to their advantage and set up a battery of cannon at the mouth of the Schuylkill River to fire on the unprotected side of the fort. British warships approached from the south and also bombarded the fort. The Americans held the meager fortifications during these bombardments, successfully destroying two British men-of-war. The British temporarily withdrew their fleet.

Washington ordered the men at the fort to hold at all cost. Every day the Americans were able to hold the river defenses delayed the much needed supplies from reaching the British in Philadelphia. Without these supplies the British could not wage an attack against Washington's main army. If the British supplies could be delayed long enough, winter would set in and the campaign would be called to an end until spring, giving Washington time to reorganize his force.

On November 10th the British mounted a massive final attack on the fort. During the day, the British continuously bombarded the fort with cannon fire from both land and sea. During the night, the exhausted Americans reconstructed the walls of the fort to withstand the next day's bombardment. It was only a matter of time before the fort would fall to the British.

OLDE FORT MIFFLIN
Philadelphia, Pennsylvania

The troops at Fort Mifflin performed valiantly during the continuous five day cannonade. In the midst of the bombardment, Washington, unable to continue timely relief to the fort, issued the following orders "...the Cannon and Stores ought immediately to be removed and everything put into a disposition to remove totally at a minute's warning; but as every day that we can hold even the Island, is so much time gained, I would recommend a party to be left, who might find good Shelter, behind the ruined Works, and when they abandon, they should set fire to the Barracks and all remaining buildings." On the night of November 15, the men of Fort Mifflin were evacuated to Fort Mercer. Forty men remained behind to destroy the fort as Washington had ordered. Without Fort Mifflin, Fort Mercer could not be defended, and so it was evacuated on the 21st opening the Delaware River to British ships.

Olde Fort Mifflin

Island Road • Philadelphia, PA 19153 • 215-365-5194

Fort Mifflin has played a diverse role throughout its long military history. The fort was begun as a British fortification to protect Philadelphia before the Revolution. As early as 1772 the fort's stone walls were erected. The site chosen was an island of mud and silt separated from the river bank by a shifting, 500 foot channel (long since filled in). When the Declaration of Independence was signed, the unfinished fort on Mud Island drew attention from the people of Philadelphia. A committee to protect Philadelphia from the British, headed by Benjamin Franklin, began a emergency program to finish the fort.

Fort Mifflin was completely destroyed after the British attack during the clearing of the Delaware River defenses. In 1798, Fort Mifflin was rebuilt by order of the President of the United States, John Adams. His name can still be seen on the white keystones of the sallyport arches. The brick walls were erected atop the remnants of the stone walls of the original fort. These stone walls may still be seen, facing the river.

In the War of 1812, Fort Mifflin was manned, but did not see action when the British fleet stood off Delaware Bay. The fort was repaired and enlarged during the Civil War. Its garrison was drawn largely from two Philadelphia neighborhood units, the Kensington Rifles and the Richmond Artillery. Many Union army deserters were executed on the parade ground, and Confederate prisoners were held at the fort. Frames of bunks in which the prisoners slept are still in some of the chambers. Ammunition was stored in the fort during World War I, an anti-aircraft battery occupied it during World War II, and it was used for storage during the Korean conflict.

In 1962, the Federal government gave the City of Philadelphia title to the old fort. Today the fort is operated by the Olde Fort Mifflin Historical Society, Inc. which is in the process of restoring the fort to its early glory.

RESOURCES

Post revolutionary fort: barracks; artillery shed; powder magazine; military reenactments; special events.

TOUR INFORMATION

Visitors touring the fort will see the Olde Fort Mifflin Garrison in action. An American Revolutionary reenactment group presents life of the Colonial soldier performing daily routines. Guided tours are scheduled throughout the day, but visitors may tour the facility on a self-guided basis. Educational booklets and literature are available. Groups tours can be arranged in advance.

EDUCATIONAL PROGRAMS

Members of the Olde Fort Mifflin Garrison are available to give lectures, slide programs and reenactments for area schools and community groups. Advance reservations required. A fee is charged for these programs.

FOOD SERVICE

Picnicking is allowed on the grounds. Soda and snacks are available from the Store House.

ADMISSION

Adults $ .50; children $ .25.

HOURS

Saturday & Sunday, Noon to 5:00 p.m.
Closed December through February.

LOCATION & PARKING

Adjacent to Philadelphia Airport on Delaware River. Vehicle and bus parking outside fort entrance. For information and reservations call the fort on weekends only.

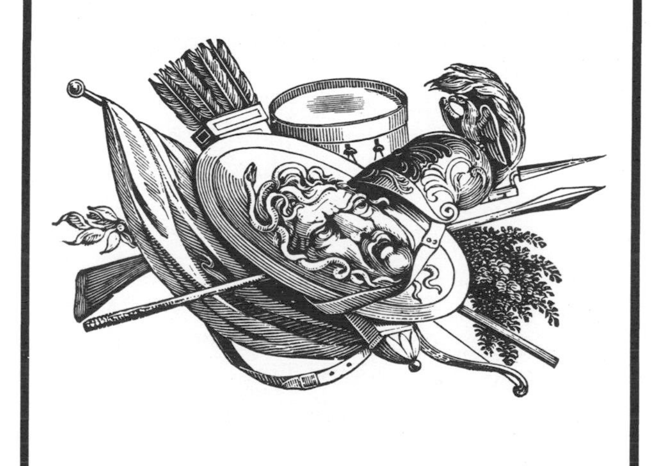

December 19, 1777

Washington & 12,000 Continentals Winter at Valley Forge

After the American defeats at Brandywine, Germantown, Forts Mifflin and Mercer, and the loss of Philadelphia to the British, Washington ordered an end to the unsuccessful Philadelphia Campaign. Washington selected Valley Forge, named for an iron forge located on the Valley Creek, as the site for the winter encampment. Washington's officers, and especially his chief military engineer, General Louis Duportail, considered Valley Forge an ideal encampment site. Only eighteen miles from British held Philadelphia, Valley Forge was far enough from the city to prevent a surprise British attack and close enough to limit British foraging in the Pennsylvania farmland. High ground made it easily defendable, and it was thought that the surrounding farmland would ensure a steady source of food supplies for the American army.

A light snow covered the ground on December 19, 1777, when Washington's ill-equipped army, weary from the long campaign, struggled into Valley Forge. Cold winds blew as the 12,000 Continentals prepared for the winter. Immediately, plans were initiated to make permanent quarters. In the meantime, tents were used to shelter the men. Grounds for brigade encampments were selected, and defense lines were planned and begun. Within days of the army's arrival, the Schuylkill River, along the camp's northern boundary, was covered by ice. Snow was six inches deep.

VALLEY FORGE NATIONAL HISTORICAL PARK

Valley Forge, Pennsylvania

English and Welsh Quakers and Baptists were the first to settle at Valley Forge in the beginning of the 18th century. The area was then known as Mount Joy. These early settlers farmed, raised livestock, and grew flax used for clothing production. With the addition of the "Mount Joy Forge" which was later known as the "Valley Forge," the area became a self-sustaining economic community. The forge made pig iron into wrought iron, as well as finished metal products. A sawmill, gristmill, and company store provided other necessary products to the community.

When war broke out in the thirteen colonies, the Valley Forge became an important source of supply for the Continental army. Shovels, horseshoes, tomahawks, and ax heads were made at the forge for the troops. The rich valley also supplied flour to the army, processed at the Valley Forge gristmill.

Valley Forge National Historical Park

P.O. Box 953 • Valley Forge, Pennsylvania 19481 • 215-783-7700

Valley Forge National Historical Park is visited annually by thousands of enthusiastic visitors. More than two hundred years prior to the picnickers, bicyclers and students of history arrived, the Continental army held its historic 1777-78 winter encampment in this area. Under the command of General George Washington, the diverse Colonial army was transformed into a unified professional fighting force that winter.

After the army's six month encampment, the Valley Forge area reverted to private use. One hundred years later in 1878 the Centennial and Memorial Association acquired Washington's Headquarters as a public memorial of the encampment. In 1893 the Pennsylvania State legislature passed an act to "...preserve, and maintain forever the revolutionary camp ground at Valley Forge."

On July 4, 1976, President Ford signed legislation establishing Valley Forge as a National Historical Park. The park passed from the control of the Commonwealth of Pennsylvania to the control of the Federal Government. It was fitting that this area became a National Park by Presidential action during the nation's Bicentennial.

Visitors can enjoy the park in a number of ways. The visitor center is the recommended first stop. Here a film and exhibits orient visitors before they tour the park. A self-guided auto tour or a bus tour (available during summer months) is an excellent way for visitors to experience Valley Forge. Others hike, bicycle, ride horses, or cross-country ski through the park. Historical buildings including Washington's Headquarters and General Varnum's Quarters are open to the public. Park Service staff in period costume carry out soldier life demonstrations throughout the year. The expanded summer program often includes special interpretive activities.

RESOURCES

Restored historic buildings; reconstructed huts and redoubts; artillery park; Visitor Center — exhibits, audio-visual program, bookstore; bus tours (April-Oct.); recreational areas; nature trails; special events.

VISITOR CENTER

Tours start at the Visitor Center. An audio-visual program and exhibits, including Washington's sleeping marquee, on loan from the Valley Forge Historical Society, introduce visitors to the story of the 1777-78 winter encampment. The park staff will help visitors plan their visit.

EDUCATIONAL PROGRAMS

Soldier Life: The Revolutionary Soldier; *America in Rebellion: The War Years*; *George Washington: The Soldier, the Man*; *Small Things Forgotten: Exploring Material Culture* are educational programs offered free to school groups, grades 3 through 12. All programs begin at 11:00 a.m. and teachers are encouraged to allow time to tour the park and the Visitor Center. Pre-visit materials are provided for classroom use. Call for reservations.

TOUR INFORMATION

A self-guided driving route through the park includes stops at numerous historic sites. Pick up an interpretive map at the visitor center. A narrated bus tour is available April 15—October 31; a fee is charged. A taped narrative tour of the park is available for rent or purchase. Guided tours are not offered.

LIBRARY

The Horace "Vos" Willcox Library contains over 3,000 volumes on Valley Forge and the American Revolution. Call for information.

FOOD SERVICE

A snack bar is available at the Washington's Headquarters area of the park. Advance reservations for groups are helpful, call 215-783-9958.

ADMISSION

Free

HOURS

Daily, 8:30 a.m. to 5:00 p.m. Closed Christmas Day.

LOCATION & PARKING

The Visitor Center is located at the intersection of Route 23 and North Gulph Rd. just off the 422 Expressway. Vehicle and bus parking available throughout the park.

February 25, 1778

Washington Reorganizes Army: Gen. Greene Quarter Master

Shortly after the army arrived at Valley Forge, construction began on permanent quarters for the long winter months ahead. Trees from the surrounding forests were cut and used to build huts for the men. Within a month almost all of the men moved from tents into log huts. This temporary community was divided into sections for each of the fifteen brigades following the fashion of "proper streets." The total area of the encampment was nearly two thousand acres.

Through the winter, critical shortages of food and clothing plagued the army. Transportation contributed to the problem as well as the lack of an organized Quartermaster department, the division of the army responsible for providing food and supplies to the men. Soldiers received irregular supplies of meat and bread, often getting their only nourishment from "firecake," a bland mixture of flour and water. So severe were conditions that Washington impressed by the determination of his troops wrote: "...we cannot enough admire the incomparable patience and fidelity of the American Soldiery." Almost two thousand died of typhus, typhoid, dysentery, and other diseases.

In March, General Nathanael Greene, one of Washington's most trusted and competent officers, accepted the post of Quartermaster General. In the months that followed, problems of supply and transportation were steadily resolved under Greene's leadership.

Washington Seeks Supplies for Army

By Virtue of the Power and direction of Me especially given, I hearby enjoin and require all Persons residing within seventy Miles of my Head Quarters to thresh one Half of their Grain by the 1st Day of February, and the other Half by the 1st Day of March next ensuing, on Pain, in Case of Failure, of having all that shall remain in Sheaves after the Period above mentioned, seized by the Commissaries and Quarter-Masters of the Army, and paid for as Straw.

GIVEN under my Hand, at Quarters, near the Valley forge, in Philadelphia County, this 20th Day of December, 1777.
— G. Washington.

From Washington's Orders at Valley Forge.

February 23, 1778

Von Steuben Arrives: Develops Manual of Arms

Upgrading military efficiency, morale, and discipline was as vital to the well-being of the army as securing a reliable system of supply. Field manuals were books of military drill, movement, and strategies. While the soldiers were trained, not all companies used the same field manual. This lack of uniformity had handicapped the American force in battle and had made coordinated battle movements awkward. The task of developing and carrying out an effective training program fell to Baron Friedrich von Steuben, a veteran of the Prussian army of Frederick the Great. Von Steuben arrived at Valley Forge in February.

Numerous obstacles threatened von Steuben's efforts. No American field manual had been written, morale was low, and von Steuben only spoke a little English. Undaunted, he drafted a new manual in French. His aides, often working late into the night, translated his work into English. Each day he would introduce a new exercise to Washington's Life Guard, his model company, who, in turn, trained the rest of the army.

From dawn to dusk von Steuben worked directly with the men, a break from tradition, forming them into an effective, uniform fighting force. Soon, the troops moved smartly from line to column and column to line, loaded muskets with precision, and drove imaginary redcoats from the field by skillful charges with the bayonet. Through von Steuben's efforts the army was transformed from individuals into an effective uniform fighting force, a match for any professional army.

The Importance of Leadership

The American Continental troops are very war-wise and quite well disciplined. They are thoroughly inured to hardship, which they endure with little complaint so long as their officers set them an example, but it is imperative that the officers equal their troops in firmness and resolution. They have supreme confidence in General Washington...

From a commentary by the Frenchman, Jean-Baptiste-Antoine de Verger, Royal Deux-Points Regiment, Yorktown, Virginia, 1781.

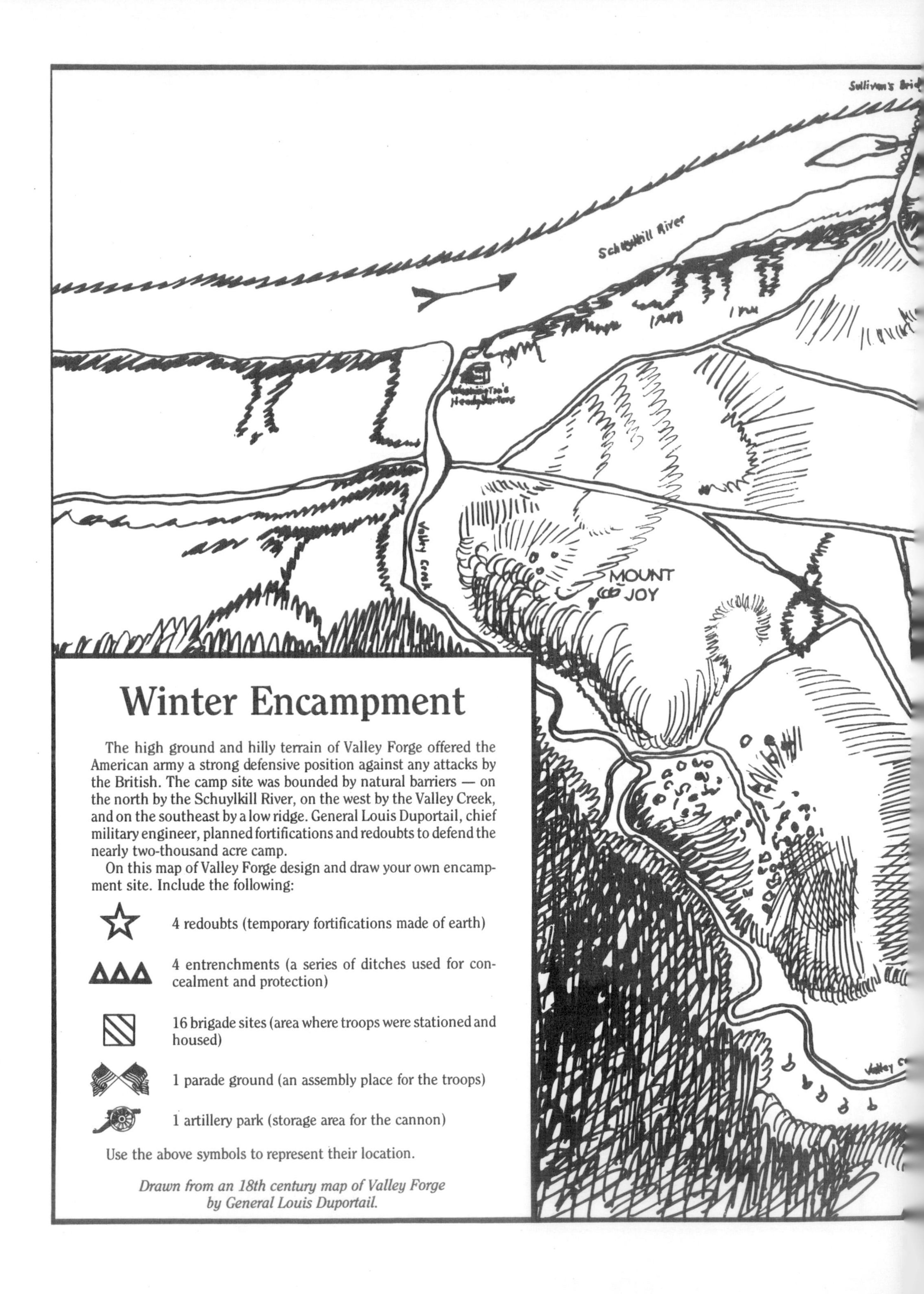

Winter Encampment

The high ground and hilly terrain of Valley Forge offered the American army a strong defensive position against any attacks by the British. The camp site was bounded by natural barriers — on the north by the Schuylkill River, on the west by the Valley Creek, and on the southeast by a low ridge. General Louis Duportail, chief military engineer, planned fortifications and redoubts to defend the nearly two-thousand acre camp.

On this map of Valley Forge design and draw your own encampment site. Include the following:

☆ 4 redoubts (temporary fortifications made of earth)

△△△ 4 entrenchments (a series of ditches used for concealment and protection)

▧ 16 brigade sites (area where troops were stationed and housed)

1 parade ground (an assembly place for the troops)

1 artillery park (storage area for the cannon)

Use the above symbols to represent their location.

Drawn from an 18th century map of Valley Forge by General Louis Duportail.

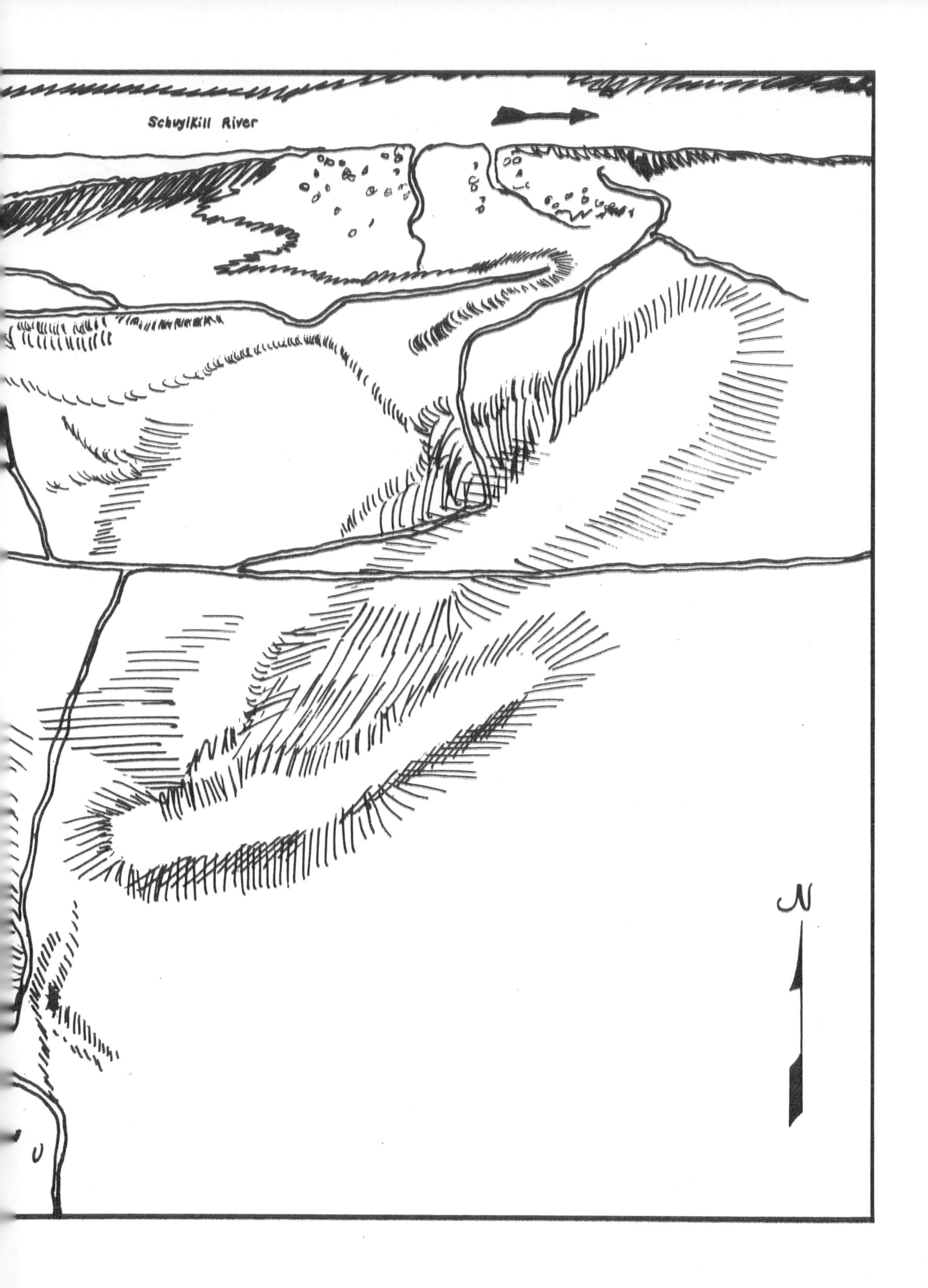
Schuylkill River
N

May 4, 1778, *York, PA*
Congress ratifies treaties with France.

May 8, 1778, *Philadelphia, PA*
Howe relieved of duty, Sir Henry Clinton to replace him.

May 20, 1778, *Valley Forge, PA*
Former prisoner Gen. Lee arrives at Valley Forge.

May 6, 1778

Army at Valley Forge Celebrates French-American Alliance

On May 1, 1778 unofficial news came to Valley Forge that France had signed a "Treaty of Amity and Commerce" and a "Treaty of Military Alliance" with the United States. Many believed that this important event would secure lasting independence for America.

Washington set aside May 6th as a day of celebration by the army at Valley Forge. In the morning a cannon was fired as a signal for the fifteen brigades to assemble on the Grand Parade, the centrally located, open training ground. After a discharge of thirteen cannon, the infantry began a running fire of their muskets down the front line, then down the second line. Three firings were each followed by huzzas and a toast—"long live the King of France—long live the Friendly European powers—Huzza to the American States."

A soldier at Valley Forge described the scene: "The exact order in which the columns marched to their ground—the celerity and precision with which the lines were formed—the regularity of the fire—the pillars of fleecy smoke ascending in rapid succession—the continued sound of the musquetry, not unlike the rolling of distant thunder—conspired to exhibit a magnificent scene of joy, worthy of the great occasion."

Secret support from France had come before this time, but the French-American Alliance assured the United States of open and continuing support. The French sent military supplies such as muskets, cannon, ammunition, and uniforms. They also offered money to the United States and gave the assistance of their army and navy.

VALLEY FORGE HISTORICAL SOCIETY

Valley Forge, Pennsylvania

Overlooking the Grand Parade where von Steuben trained the Continental Army and where the French Alliance was celebrated on May 6th, 1778 is the renowned Washington Memorial. This imposing gothic structure was begun as a religious and patriotic memorial by the Rev. Mr. W. Herbert Burk in 1903. Today the memorial houses the Valley Forge Historical Society Museum, the Washington Memorial Library, and the Washington Memorial Chapel and Carillon.

Built to honor the dedication and sacrifice of George Washington and the men of Valley Forge,

this is truly a national memorial, as Rev. Burk raised building funds from visitors and patriotic contributors from all parts of the United States. The Washington Memorial continues to attract thousands of visitors annually.

Valley Forge Historical Society

P.O. Box 122 • Valley Forge, Pennsylvania 19481 • 215-783-0535

The Valley Forge Historical Society was founded as the patriotic arm of the Washington Memorial. Its museum was begun in 1918 to house the Reverend Mr. W. H. Burk's growing collection of artifacts relating to George Washington and the American Revolution.

The Society recently renovated its museum and opened an exciting new exhibit, "Valley Forge: The Reality and the Symbol." This permanent exhibit was designed to highlight the Historical Society's priceless holdings and to tell the story of the encampment in a graphic and dramatic manner.

The "Reality" section depicts the pre-encampment periods including the settlement of the area by English and Welsh Quakers under William Penn and the coming of war in the fall of 1777. It also highlights events of the Valley Forge encampment including the arrival of the army in December, winter hardships, military preparation in the spring, and the army's departure in June, 1778.

The "Symbol" area ingeniously traces the gradual development of George Washington and Valley Forge as historic symbols through 200 years of American history using a varied collection of art and artifacts.

The Museum's Martha Washington Gallery displays the Society's Washington Collection, the third largest and finest collection of Washington artifacts and memorabilia in the United States. Changing exhibits in this gallery display historical china, engraved powder horns, samplers, prints, and fine firearms.

Among the priceless collection held by the Society are: Washington's sleeping tent (on loan for display to the Valley Forge National Historical Park); his Commander-in-Chief's flag—blue silk with thirteen six-pointed stars; and the famous painting *The March to Valley Forge* by William B. T. Trego.

RESOURCES
Museum; interpretive exhibits; museum shop; special events.

MUSEUM
The Museum contains a priceless collection of more than 4,000 items illustrating George Washington, Revolutionary War life, and artifacts that document Valley Forge as a symbol of patriotism.

EDUCATIONAL PROGRAMS
Special educational tours are available with advance reservations. They include: "A Valley Forge Adventure," museum exploratory sheets for elementary, middle, or senior high students; a "hands-on" treasure chest of artifacts; and the opportunity to try on reproduction colonial clothing.

TOUR INFORMATION
Individuals tour the Museum's exhibit areas on a self-guided basis. In addition to the artifacts on display, interpretive graphics and labels aid the visitor in understanding the themes presented. Interpretive brochures are available for a small fee. Guided tours are available to school groups with advance reservations. Call for information and reservations.

LIBRARY
The Washington Memorial Library contains several hundred volumes on George Washington and the American Revolution. Open by appointment only.

ADMISSION
Adults $ 1.00 donation; children 10 & under free; groups free.

HOURS
Monday—Saturday, 9:30 a.m. to 4:30 p.m. Sunday, 1:00 p.m. to 4:30 p.m.

LOCATION & PARKING
Washington Memorial complex adjacent to Valley Forge National Historical Park on Route 23. Vehicle and bus parking on site grounds.

ADDITIONAL SITES
The **Washington Memorial Chapel** is a parish of the Episcopal Church. The public is welcome to visit this memorial to George Washington. All services are open to the general public. For information call 215-783-0120.

American Revolutionary Crossword Puzzle

ACROSS CLUES

2. A spear like weapon about 6-6½ feet long used by officers during the Revolution.
4. Betsy Ross sewed one of these during the Revolution.
7. General who led the American forced during the Revolution.
10. Accurate firearm used by snipers and sharpshooters.
11. A bag used by soldiers to carry their supplies.
13. A sword-like attachment mounted on the end of a musket or rifle.
14. The title awarded to all soldiers in an army, such as private, captain, general.
15. Many soldiers wore a tricorne ________.
18. Temporary shelter used by the men of both armies as they traveled from place to place.
19. Another name for cannon.
24. ________ and drums were played during battle to signal the troops.
25. When soldiers were not staying in Forts or barracks they would ________ in tents.
26. Log ________ were constructed to protect the soldiers during the cold winters.
27. The principal firearm carried by both American and British soldiers during the Revolution. This was not a very accurate weapon.
29. A handgun carried primarily by officers during the Revolution.
30. A holder for a dagger, bayonet or sword.

DOWN CLUES

1. Soldiers who rode into battle on horseback.
3. A container used by soldiers to hold gunpowder.
5. Foot soldiers were called ________ men.
6. A colonist who supported the British during the Revolution.
8. A hachet used by soldiers and Indians during the Revolution.
9. A paper cylinder that holds the lead ball and powder charge that would be loaded into a musket.
12. A container that soldiers use for carrying water.
16. A stone that sparks when struck by metal.
17. Pants worn by soldiers during the Revolution.
20. Armies were divided into smaller groups called ________.
21. A highest ranking officer in both the American and British Armies.
22. A drawing of the landscape and terrain used as a directional guide and to plan battles.
23. A person who provides secret information about the enemy.
24. A large structure built to defend an area against enemy attack.
28. Boys too young to fight could join the army to play the ________ for the troops.

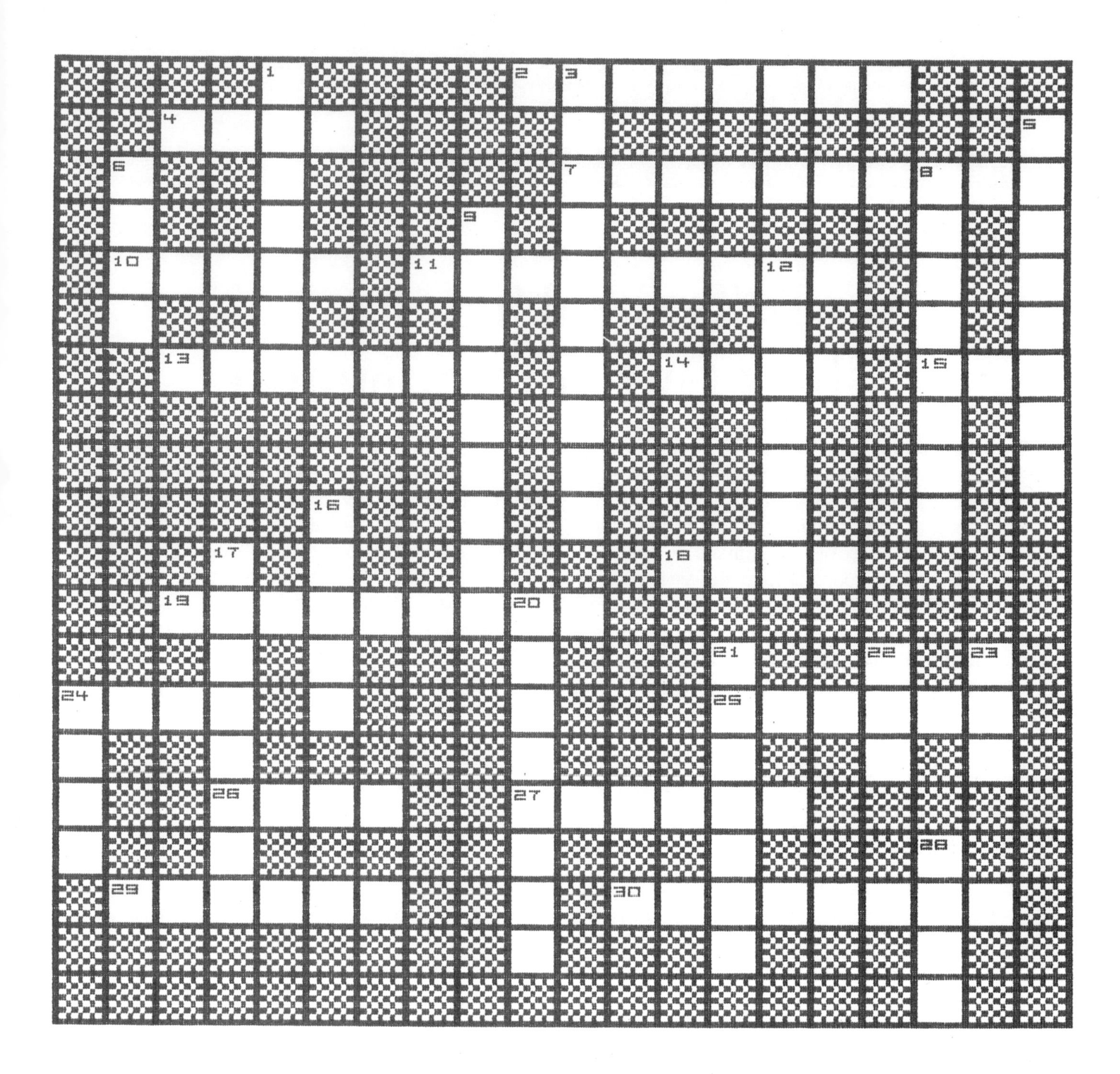

WORD LIST:

ARTILLERY
BAYONET
BREECHES
CALVARY
CARTRIDGE
CANTEEN
DRUM
ENCAMP
FIFE
FLAG
FLINT
FORT
GENERAL
HAVERSACK
HAT
HUTS
INFANTRY
MAP
MUSKET
PISTOL
POWDERHORN
RANK
REGIMENT
RIFLE
SCABBARD
SPONTOON
SPY
TENT
TORY
TOMAHAWK
WASHINGTON

ANSWERS

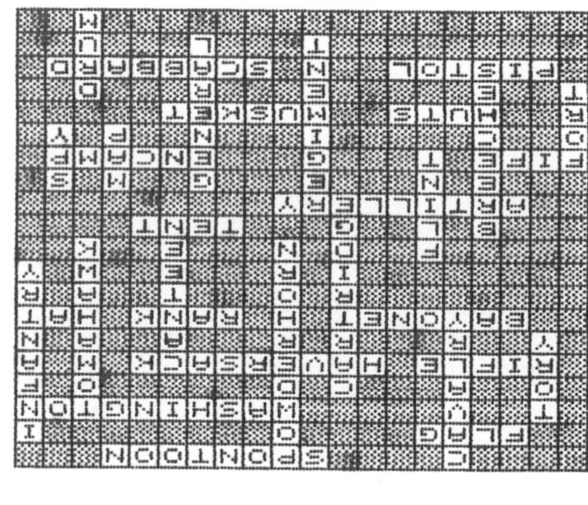

June 6, 1778, *Philadelphia, PA*
The Carlisle Peace Commission arrives in Philadelphia bearing proposals for conciliation.

June 17, 1778, *York, PA*
Congress rejects proposals of conciliation, demands British withdrawal and independence.

June 19, 1778, *Valley Forge, PA*
Americans march out of Valley Forge in pursuit of the British.

June 28, 1778

Newly Trained Troops Hold Their Own at Monmouth

With the coming of spring, 1778 Britain found itself fighting both the Colonies and France. Lieutenant General Sir Henry Clinton was ordered to Philadelphia to take command of the British force relieving William Howe of his command. In an effort to concentrate their troops, Britain ordered the evacuation of Philadelphia. On May 23rd word arrived directing Clinton to move the army to New York. Washington with his army at Valley Forge received word almost immediately and planned to block the British march to New York. By the 18th of June Clinton had successfully moved over 10,000 troops and numerous supplies out of Philadelphia into New Jersey. The patriots regained their lost capital city without firing a shot.

Washington called a council of war on June 24th to establish a strategy against Clinton and his men. Charles Lee and his supporters were against engaging the British professional troops in a major engagement. Others such as Greene, Wayne, von Steuben, and LaFayette favored a major offensive action against the British, believing that the troops were more than prepared to take on the British after their extensive training at Valley Forge. The council concluded recommending that the army avoid a major confrontation. Washington sent a small number of troops out to harass the enemy's right and left flank. As the British approached Monmouth, Washington realized he needed to reinforce his men in the field.

MONMOUTH BATTLEFIELD STATE PARK

Freehold, New Jersey

With the British in Freehold, Washington arrived in nearby Englishtown and ordered his generals to attack the British on the morning of the 28th as they resumed their march. General Lee with an advance force remained reluctant to attack the British, but was drawn into battle by the British. In the confusion Lee ordered his troops to retreat. Washington, furious with this state of affairs, took command of the troops and organized the troops in a defensive position. For the remainder of the day the two armies clashed in the unbearably hot weather, finally withdrawing at 5 o'clock from exhaustion.

Washington planned to resume the battle the next day, but shortly after midnight, Clinton and his men slipped away undetected by Washington's army. Neither side emerged as a winner in the Battle, but the Americans had proven themselves as a professional fighting force.

Monmouth Battlefield State Park

RD 1, Box 258 • Freehold, New Jersey 07728 • 201-462-9616

Visitors to Monmouth Battlefield State Park can walk along the grounds of the park, recalling the hot summer day of June 28th 1778 when the American and British forces clashed under the direction of General George Washington and General Sir Henry Clinton. Visitors can stroll down the Combs Hill, where Washington's cannons were placed, to a bridge crossing the morass (low-lying soggy ground) and walk on the battlefield itself. The presence of Washington, LaFayette, von Steuben, "Mad" Anthony Wayne, Molly Pitcher, and other colorful personalities of the period at this important battle further contributes to the historic significance of the site. The 1500 acre wooded area features a historic marker and monuments commemorating the events of the battle. The area has been placed on the National and State registers of historic places.

During the battle, many local residents were involved in the fighting or had their homes taken over and used as hospitals or headquarters. One of these people was John Craig of Freehold. John Craig, who was paymaster for the local militia, was involved in the action at Monmouth. His wife and family remained behind on their farm.

Reports reached Mrs. Craig that the British were marching toward her farm, so she packed her children and two slaves into a wagon and fled. Some say the Craig's house was used as a temporary field hospital by the British during the battle.

The Craig House, located in Monmouth Battlefield State Park, was built in 1710 and has been restored to its 18th Century appearance. The house has four rooms, three fireplaces and a cold cellar downstairs. There are four bedrooms upstairs. Above the kitchen is a small sleeping area that served as slave quarters.

RESOURCES
Visitor Center; audio-visual orientation program; exhibit; bookstore; historic house; battlefield; playground; playing fields; trails; special events.

VISITOR CENTER & HISTORIC HOUSE
Two slide programs, a topographical map utilizing optic fiber lights, and an interpretive exhibit provide visitors with an understanding of the Battle of Monmouth. The 18th century Craig House interprets farm life during the time of the Revolution.

TOUR INFORMATION
Visitors tour the visitor's center and grounds on a self-guided basis. Guided tours of the Craig House are available. Reservations are required for large groups visiting the site.

FOOD SERVICE
Two picnic areas are available for public use. A food service is operated on Saturday, Sunday, and holidays during the summer.

ADMISSION
Free

HOURS
Visitor Center
Daily, 9:00 a.m. to 4:00 p.m.

Craig House
Summer & fall: Thursday—Sunday, 10:00 a.m. to 5:00 p.m. Winter & spring: Saturday & Sunday, 10:00 a.m. to 5:00 p.m.

LOCATION & PARKING
Visitor Center on Route 33, West of Freehold, NJ.
Craig House at Shibanoff Road, West of Route 9, North of Route 33 circle.

MOLLY PITCHER AT THE BATTLE OF MONMOUTH

The Monmouth County Historical Association

70 Court Street • Freehold, New Jersey 07728 • 201-462-1466

The Monmouth County Historical Association was founded in 1898 to collect, preserve and interpret materials related to the region's heritage. Since its beginning, the Association has developed into a leading local historical organization and has made its museum and research collections available to the public. These resources are displayed in a modern museum building and four historic houses.

The Georgian style museum was built as the Association's headquarters and library in 1931. Exceptional collections of furniture, paintings and decorative arts of all periods, most of which were owned or made in New Jersey, are displayed. Special holdings include English and Chinese ceramics, folk art, children's toys and items relating to local history. Two of the more significant items representing the American Revolution are the painting *Washington at Monmouth* by Emanuel Leutze and a dispatch from Major C. R. Hunter to General Washington regarding troop movements prior to the Battle of Monmouth.

Four early county houses are owned and operated by the Monmouth County Historical Association. The **Covenhoven House** was built in 1752 in Freehold and was probably the first example of a house built in the county in the Georgian style of architecture. The Covenhovens were wealthy farmers and the house has been furnished according to the 1790 inventory of their estate. **Marlpit Hall** in Middletown was begun in 1685 as a one-room Dutch cottage and enlarged in the English style about 1740 by John Taylor, a Tory merchant. After the Revolution, the house remained in the Taylor family until restored by the Association in 1936. **Allen House** in Shrewsbury was operated as the Blue Ball Tavern for much of the late 18th century. Two rooms are furnished as a tavern and the other areas provide changing exhibits on County history. **Holmes-Hendrickson House** in Holmdel reflects local Dutch building traditions of the 18th century.

RESOURCES

Museum and Library; restored and furnished historic houses; special events.

MUSEUM

The Museum serves as the headquarters of the Association, and houses the library as well as the Association's extensive collections.

EDUCATIONAL PROGRAMS

A wide variety of outstanding educational programs are available for both elementary and secondary students at the museum, library, and historic houses. Call for information.

EDUCATIONAL MATERIALS

Outreach packets are available for loan to teachers of grades 3 to 12. The packets contain slides, background information, activities, and work sheets. A fee is charged. Call the Education Coordinator Tuesdays, Thursdays, or Fridays for information.

TOUR INFORMATION

Guided tours of the Museum and historic properties are available for the general public and adult groups. School groups are required to participate in the educational programs available. Call for reservations.

LIBRARY & ARCHIVES

The research library and archives contain an outstanding collection on regional history and genealogy. Student groups conducting research are welcome with advance reservations.

ADMISSION

Adults $ 1.00; seniors $ .75; children $ .50, under 6 free; groups of 20 or more $ .75.

Admission charged at each facility.

HOURS

Museum

Tuesday—Saturday, 10:00 a.m. to 4:00 p.m.
Sunday 1:00 p.m. to 4:00 p.m.

Library & Archives

Wednesday—Saturday, 10:00 a.m. to 4:00 p.m. Call for information regarding the historic houses.

LOCATION & PARKING

70 Court Street, in the center of Freehold, NJ, near the Court House and directly across from the Monmouth Battle Monument. Buses may park in front of the Museum.

Women & the American Revolution

Women, as well as men, offered their support to the American cause during the Revolution. Many women stayed at home running the family farm or business and offered support as they could. Less fortunate women lost their homes to the enemy. Many of these homeless women and children followed the troops gaining the term "camp followers." They served the army as nurses, laundresses, cooks, and seamstresses, even taking up arms when needed.

One of the most heroic of these women was Molly Hays known generally today as Molly Pitcher. On the unbearably hot day of the Battle of Monmouth, Molly was aiding her husband and his fellow gunners by bringing water to them as they fired their cannon. As she returned with more water she discovered that her husband William Hays had fallen in battle. She immediately took his place, serving as a gunner for the remainder of the battle. Legend has it that Molly was presented to General Washington after the battle.

Instructions

The story of Molly Pitcher has been romanticized in many paintings and engravings since the Revolution. On the following page draw your own version of Molly Pitcher's role in the Battle of Monmouth. Include the following characters and elements: Molly Pitcher, George Washington, George Washington's horse, soldiers, a cannon, a flag, and a water container. You may add other elements if you wish.

Molly Pitcher at the Battle of Monmouth
by

____

December 11, 1778

Americans Winter In Middlebrook

On December 11, 1778, Washington and his army arrived in Middlebrook, New Jersey, near Bound Brook. Washington was preparing his troops for winter and once again selected the safety of the Watchung Mountains for his winter encampment. The American Army could keep a watchful eye on the British in New York, and the mountains offered protection against a British attack.

The winter of 1778-1779 proved to be a mild one. Diversions for the army during the encampment included many balls and assemblies. Spring brought the arrival of the French Minister, M. Girard, and his companion, the Minister of Spain, Don Juan Miralles. Girard pledged continued French support along with an increase in supplies and men to further aid the Americans against the British. The Delaware Indians also visited Washington in mid-May, *en route* from Philadelphia where they had met with Congress. Washington warned them against becoming hostile to the American cause. They in turn presented Washington with a memorial reiterating their support for the Americans. Washington held a review in their honor. Camp broke shortly after this on June 3rd.

WALLACE HOUSE
Somerville, New Jersey

John Wallace, a Philadelphia tea merchant, purchased land and a small house in the Middlebrook area of New Jersey in 1775. Between 1775 and 1778 Wallace built an eight room addition onto the original structure. This new house, the largest built at that time in the Raritan Valley, was nearing completion when it was appropriated as headquarters for General Washington in November, 1778. Besides being large and commodious, it had the added convenience of not yet being occupied by the Wallace family. With Washington's rental of the house, Wallace and his family remained in Philadelphia until camp broke in June of 1779.

After spending Christmas in Philadelphia and a month attending Congress, Washington returned to the Middlebrook camp. He arrived at Wallace's home in February accompanied by his wife, Martha, aides, and several servants.

Wallace House & Old Dutch Parsonage

38 Washington Place • Somerville, NJ 08876 • 201-725-1015

Located near the center of Somerville, the Wallace House and Old Dutch Parsonage serve to remind visitors and the local community of the significant role the area played in the events of the American Revolution. The two properties are located on a quiet residential street only a few hundred feet from each other. Today these properties are maintained and managed by the New Jersey Department of Environmental Protection, Division of Parks and Forestry, and they are open to the public on a regular basis.

The Old Dutch Parsonage, which originally was located three-quarters of a mile to the east of the Wallace House was built in 1751 for Reverend John Frelinghuysen and his wife, Dinah Van Berg. Shortly after starting a seminary in the Parsonage, Frelinghuysen died, leaving his widow alone with two children. One of the students of the seminary, Jacob Hardenberg married Dinah. He was the first minister ordained in the Dutch Reformed Church to have been educated in America. He and Dinah lived in the Parsonage, but in 1766, the school was moved to New Brunswick, where it became known as Queens College and later Rutgers University.

During the Revolution, Hardenberg was a staunch Patriot and good friend of the Washingtons. There are numerous references to the Washingtons and Hardenbergs visiting each other during the winter of 1778-79 when the Washingtons were headquartered in the nearby Wallace House.

In 1907 the Jersey Central Railroad Company purchased the property intending to demolish the Parsonage. Joseph Frelinghuysen, a descendant of the minister, purchased the house from the railroad company and in 1914, had it moved to its present location.

RESOURCES
Restored & furnished 18th century house; special events; museum shop.

TOUR INFORMATION
A staff member or volunteer escorts groups or individuals through the Wallace House on a one hour tour. Advance reservations required for group tours. Call for reservations.

ADMISSION
Free

HOURS
Wednesday—Friday, 9:00 a.m. to Noon & 1:00 p.m. to 5:00 p.m. Saturday, 10:00 a.m. to Noon & 1:00 p.m. to 5:00 p.m. Sunday, 1:00 p.m. to 5:00 p.m. Closed Thanksgiving, Christmas & New Year's Day.

LOCATION & PARKING
38 Washington Place only a few blocks from downtown Somerville. Parking is available next to the Wallace House.

July 14, 1780

Washington Receives News: French Forces Arrive

After Washington's long hard winter encampment at Morristown in 1780 and the ensuing battle at Springfield, New Jersey, Washington brought his army to the vicinity of the Passaic Falls. Washington established his Headquarters at the home of patriot Theunis Dey while the brigades were assigned to camp sites along the Passaic River and behind the surrounding hills. From July 1st to July 29th the army maintained this strategic position near British-held New York City. Abundant food supplies and forage kept the army well fed.

On July 14th Washington received the heartening news that the French allies, over 5,000 men, had landed in Newport, Rhode Island to aid the American cause. Dispatch riders dashed away from the Dey Mansion with letters from Washington, one with a letter of notification to Congress, and another with a greeting of welcome to the French Commander, the Count de Rochambeau. After establishing a meeting with Rochambeau, Washington left the Dey Mansion on July 30th.

During the next several months Washington and the army campaigned in the Hudson Highlands. At the end of September, Benedict Arnold's treasonous plan to turn over the Fort at West Point to the British was revealed. Washington again needed a safe haven, so he returned to the Dey Mansion on October 8, 1780. Until the end of November Washington remained at the Dey Mansion dealing with treason within his own ranks, planning strategy against the British, and keeping a watchful eye on their camp in New York.

THE DEY MANSION
Wayne, New Jersey

The Dey Mansion in Preakness (now Wayne, NJ), was the home of Theunis Dey during the American Revolution. Theunis Dey, a fourth generation Dutch-American was a Bergen County Freeholder who in 1777 was selected to lead the county militia. In response, Dey offered the eastern portion of his mansion to Washington to be used as he saw fit. Washington took advantage of this generous offer and established his headquarters here on two occasions, once in July and then again in October and November, 1780.

Washington's stay at the Dey Mansion was an eventful one. Time was spent developing new strategies with the French, working with committees from Congress, and meeting and entertaining important dignitaries. Washington remarked in later years that the army was never better fed nor clothed than at the encampment at the Dey Mansion.

The Dey Mansion

199 Totowa Road • Wayne, New Jersey 07470 • 201-696-1776

The Dey Mansion, one of the finest examples of pre-revolutionary Georgian architecture in America, was built by Dirck Dey around 1740. His son, Theunis, inherited the estate, and in 1749 brought his bride Hester Schuyler to the manor house where their ten children were born. Five of their sons served in the military during the War for Independence.

Theunis Dey served with distinction as a member of the Board of Chosen Freeholders of Bergen County and a member of the State Assembly and Council. He was appointed Colonel of the Bergen County Militia in January 1777.

Theunis and Hester Dey died shortly after the end of the Revolutionary War. The Dey heirs disposed of their family's ancestral seat in 1801. Since then, sixteen individuals have owned the house. When The Passaic County Park Commission took title on January 10th, 1930, only 56.3 acres of the original 600 acre farm was still part of the estate.

Restoration plans prepared for The Passaic County Park Commission by Charles Over Cornelius remained on file until late 1933 when the Civil Works Administration of the Federal Government supplied skilled artisans to complete the project. The restoration of the Dey Mansion was based upon definite evidence found in the house itself. All obvious Victorian and modern changes were removed. A conservative approach was taken with ambiguous areas waiting until definite proof could be obtained before restoration was attempted. The formal opening of the museum was celebrated on October 8, 1934. The new museum, essentially unfurnished, began a program of acquisitions which has been carried on to the present. Furniture and accessories are characteristic of the first three-quarters of the eighteenth century.

RESOURCES

Restored and furnished 18th century home; colonial gardens; barn & other out buildings; special events; picnic area.

EDUCATIONAL PROGRAMS

A slide show is available to groups on request.

EDUCATIONAL MATERIALS

Interpretive materials are available on the history and restoration of the Dey Mansion.

TOUR INFORMATION

A staff member or volunteer guides groups or individuals through the Dey Mansion on a 45 to 60 minute tour. The tour for school groups is oriented to the group's age level. Advance reservations are required for group tours. Self-guided tours of the house are not available. Visitors are encouraged to tour the grounds on their own. Call for reservations.

FOOD SERVICE

Picnicking is allowed on the grounds. Reservations required for groups.

ADMISSION

Adults $ 1.00; children 15 & under free;
group rate for adults & children, $ 1.00 per person.

HOURS

Tuesday, Wednesday & Friday, 1:00 p.m. to 4:00 p.m.; Saturday, 10:00 a.m. to Noon & 1:00 p.m. to 4:00 p.m.; Sunday, 10:00 a.m. to 4:00 p.m.

Closed Thanksgiving, Christmas & New Year's Day.

LOCATION & PARKING

Off I-80 at 199 Totowa Road, Wayne, NJ. Vehicle and bus parking on site.

NEW JERSEY

Engraving of a painting of Washington at Trenton by John Trubull

Images of George Washington

Instructions

Many portraits of George Washington have been made. A few are depicted here. See how many other portraits of Washington you can find.

These portraits give us some idea of what Washington looked like during his life. Look carefully at each portrait, and try to decide which portraits represent Washington during the various phases of his life—gentleman farmer, military hero, President, and elder statesman. Mark each portrait with your answer.

Engraving of a 1772 painting by Charles Willson Peale. The earliest known portrait of Washington.

Washington after a portrait by Rembrandt Peale.

Silhouette of Washington, 1795.

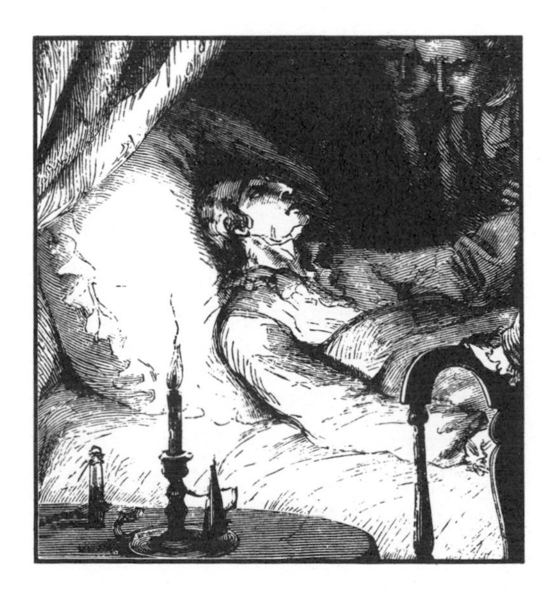

Darley's drawing of the death of Washington.

October 19, 1781, *Yorktown, VA*
Cornwallis forced to surrender after Americans and French lay siege to the city.

April 11, 1783, *Philadelphia, PA*
Congress proclaims an end to hostilities with Britain.

September 3, 1783, *Paris, France*
America and Britain sign final Peace Treaty.

November 2, 1783

Washington Writes Farewell Address To Armies

On June 30th, 1783, two years after the major American victory at Yorktown, Congress fled Independence Hall in Philadelphia because of threats to them from American troops dissatisfied because of the lack of clothing, rations, and pay. The British had not yet evacuated their troops from New York when Congress convened at Nassau Hall on the campus of Princeton University. Although the war was not officially at an end, Congress patiently awaited the signing of the Peace Treaty of Paris with England. Washington was invited to attend sessions of Congress, and adequate accommodations were sought for him. All of the available homes in Princeton were occupied by Congressmen and their servants, many forced to sleep two or three to a bed. Rockingham, located seven miles from Princeton, was for sale, and arrangements were made by Congress to rent the home for Washington. Washington arrived on August 23, 1783 with his wife, Martha, his staff, and some of his troops who pitched their tents on the front lawn.

It was here that Washington wrote his emotional and stirring "Farewell Address to the Armies." Washington ended his outstanding career as Commander-in-Chief of the Army with the surrender of his commission to Congress in Annapolis, Maryland on December 23rd. Washington did not have the luxury of returning to private life for long. In 1787 he was a delegate to the Constitutional Convention and was unanimously voted the first President of the United States, taking the oath of office on April 30, 1789.

Washington Resigns as Commander-in-Chief

November 2, 1783
Rocky Hill, New Jersey

...To conclude these his last public orders, to take his ultimate leave, in a short time, of the military character, and to bid a final adieu to the armies he has so long had the honor to command—he can only again offer in their behalf his recommendations to their grateful country, and his prayers to the god of armies. May ample justice be done them here, and may the choicest of heaven's favor both here and hereafter attend those, who under the divine auspices have secured innumerable blessings for others: with these wishes, and this benediction, the Commander in Chief is about to retire from service. The curtain of separation will soon be drawn—and the military scene to him will be closed forever.

General Washington's Farewell Orders.

Rockingham

P.O. Box 22 • Rocky Hill, New Jersey 08553 • 609-921-8835

Rockingham has an interesting history of its own, beginning in 1710 when John Harrison of Connecticut began building his house on a slope rising from the Millstone River. The New England architectural influence is easily seen in the original portion, which consisted of the dining room and upstairs study which have post and beam construction and a central chimney. The house was enlarged to four rooms in the 1730's giving it a salt box appearance. Rockingham owes its name to Judge John Berrien who purchased the house in 1735. The house was enlarged once again for his growing family. An advertisement which appeared in the "Royal Gazette" of New York City under the date of July 5, 1783, read: "FOR SALE -that very healthy and finely situated farm, 'Rockingham.'" It was described as consisting of 360 acres made up of orchards, farmland, meadows, and woodland, with a very good barn, stables, coach-house, granary, fowl house, kitchen building, smoke house and a three-room tenement house.

Widow Berrien sold the house in 1803 and during the next forty years the house had many owners. In 1872 Rockingham was purchased by David H. Mount who also bought the adjoining land which was being quarried at the time. By 1896, Rockingham was a boarding house for quarry workmen. When the main house was threatened with destruction, the Washington Headquarters Association was organized. The necessary funds were collected to purchase and move it a short distance up the hill. It was restored and landscaped, opening to visitors on August 25, 1897.

In August 1935, the Washington Headquarters Association presented the house to the State of New Jersey. To protect it from quarry blasting in 1957, the Kingston Trap Rock Co. moved it to its present site six-tenths of a mile farther up the hill and on the opposite side of the road. The historic site is administered by the New Jersey Department of Environmental Protection, Division of Parks and Forestry.

RESOURCES

Restored and furnished 18th century house; audio-visual program; museum shop; colonial gardens; special events.

EDUCATIONAL MATERIALS

A work sheet is available to school groups as a post-tour activity.

TOUR INFORMATION

A staff member will guide individuals and groups through Rockingham. Tours are adapted for school groups and may include material on Colonial games or the kitchen house. A 15 minute audio-visual orientation program offers individuals and adult groups an excellent overview of the American Revolution in New Jersey, with special emphasis on area sites. The grounds and gardens are toured on a self-guided basis. A garden guide book is available. Call for group reservations.

ADMISSION

Free

HOURS

Wednesday—Friday, 9:00 a.m. to Noon and 1:00 p.m. to 6:00 p.m. Sunday, 1:00 p.m. to 6:00 p.m. Closed Thanksgiving, Christmas & New Year's Day.

LOCATION & PARKING

On Route 518 east of Rocky Hill, NJ. Vehicle and bus parking available on site.

BIBLIOGRAPHY

Appel, David H., ed. *An Album for Americans.* New York, NY: Triangle Publications, Inc.; Crown Publishers, Inc., 1983. Contains many important documents, poems, songs, biographies, monuments, presidential portraits, paintings, drawings, and speeches important to Americans within the framework of a history of the United States.

Bell, Alfred Hoyt. *New Jersey and the Revolutionary War.* New Brunswick, NJ: Rutgers University Press, 1964.

Bergen County History Annual. *Fort Constitution and/or Fort Lee.* River Edge, NJ: Bergen County Historical Society, 1975.

Bill, Alfred Hoyt. *New Jersey and the Revolutionary War.* New Brunswick, NJ: Rutgers University Press, 1964. Discusses military matters as well as social and economic effects of the War in New Jersey. Suitable for adult or young adult readers.

Bill, Alfred Hoyt. *The Campaign of Princeton.*, NJ: Princeton University Press, 1948. Good summary of the entire campaign.

Bliven, Bruce, Jr. *The American Revolution; 1760-1783.* New York, NY: Random House, 1958. Account of the events leading up to the American Revolution and its major battles. Elementary grade level.

Boatner, Mark M., III. *Encyclopedia of the American Revolution.* New York, NY: David McKay Company, Inc., 1974. An extensive alphabetical listing of events and individuals involved in the Revolution.

Boatner, Mark M., III. *Landmarks of the American Revolution.* Harrisburg, PA: Stackpole Books, 1973. A state by state listing of interesting and important sites of the American Revolution.

Commager, Henry Steele. *The Great Declaration.* New York, NY: Eastern Acorn Press, 1982. A junior high school level book on the Declaration of Independence.

Commemorating the 200th Anniversary of the Battle of the Brandywine, September 1977. Chadds Ford, PA: Brandywine Battlefield Park Commission; Chadds Ford Historical Society, 1977. Good review of soldiers and units at the Battle of the Brandywine. Commemorative material of the Bicentennial.

Cottrell, Alden T. *The Old Barracks at Trenton.*, NJ: Old Barracks Association, 1959. A pamphlet detailing the history of the Old Barracks.

Dwyer, William M. *The Day is Ours!; November 1776-January 1777; An Inside View of the Battles of Trenton and Princeton.* New York, NY: The Viking Press, 1983. A narrative history drawn largely from primary sources—the participants tell their own story.

English, Fredrick. *General Hugh Mercer, Forgotten Hero of the American Revolution.* Princeton, NJ: Princeton University Press, 1975. Background history of General Mercer and his role in the Battle of Princeton.

Evans, R. E. *The American War of Independence.* Minneapolis, MN: Lerner Publications Co., 1977. History of the Revolution geared to 5th-9th grade levels, profusely illustrated with images from the period. (Originally published by Cambridge University Press, 1976.

BIBLIOGRAPHY

Ferris, Robert G., and Richard E. Morris. *The Signers of the Declaration of Independence*. Arlington, VA: Interpretive Publications, Inc., 1982. An overview of the Declaration of Independence story with a focus on the "Signers."

Flexner, James Thomas. *Washington, the Indispensable Man*. Boston, MA: Little, Brown & Co., 1974. A brief and dramatic biography of George Washington, condensed from five volumes. Interesting, easy reading.

Freeman, Douglas Southall. *George Washington* (7 vols.). New York, NY: Scribners, 1948-1957. The definative biography of George Washington. Excellent history of Washington's life.

Gifford, Edward S., Jr. *The American Revolution in the Delaware Valley*. Philadelphia, PA: Pennsylvania Society of the Sons of the Revolution, 1976. Good in-depth review of the campaign of 1777 and related subjects.

Goldstein, Ernest. *Let's Get Lost in a Painting*. Champaign, IL: Garrard, 1983. Detailed study of Emanuel Leutze's painting of "Washington Crossing the Delaware," demonstrating the artist's technique and his interpretation of the meaning of a historical event.

Henderson, Peter. *Campaign of Chaos...1776*. Haworth, NJ: Archives, Inc., Ltd., 1975. A chronology of the Revolutionary War along the Hudson River.

Hutton, Ann Hawkes. *George Washington Crossed Here*. Philadelphia, PA: Chilton, 1966. A history of the events of the crossing written in a style suitable for children and adults.

Hutton, Ann Hawkes. *Portrait of Patriotism*. Radnor, PA: Chilton, 1959. A biography of Emanuel Leutze, painter of the famous "Washington Crossing the Delaware." Includes a history of the creation of the painting and the crossing of the Delaware.

Hutton, Ann Hawkes. *The Year and Spirit of '76*. Radnor, PA, Chilton, 1972. A history of the year 1776 and the events leading to the crossing of the Delaware.

Jackson, John W. *Defense of the Delaware*. New Brunswick, NJ: Rutgers University Press, n.d.

Jackson, John W. *The Delaware Bay and River Defenses of Philadelphia, 1775-1777*. Philadelphia, PA: Philadelphia Maritime Museum, 1977. Concise account of the defenses of the Delaware.

Jackson, John W. *Whitemarsh 1777, Impregnable Stronghold*. Fort Washington, PA: Historical Society of Fort Washington, 1984. A well researched and written account of the role of the Whitemarsh area in the Revolution.

Jackson, John W. *With the British Army in Philadelphia*. San Rafael, CA: Presidio Press, 1979. An account of the British occupation of Philadelphia.

Judd, Jacob. *Fort Lee on the Palisades: The Battle for the Hudson*. Tarrytown, NJ: Sleepy Hollow Restoration, 1963.

Ketchum, Richard M., ed. *The World of George Washington*. New York, NY: American Heritage Publishing Company, Inc.; Harmony Books, 1974. Excellent book on the life of George Washington. Includes numerous illustrations.

BIBLIOGRAPHY

Konkle, Burton Alva. *Benjamin Chew.* Philadelphia, PA: University of Pennsylvania, 1932. Chapter XV: "The Fall of Philadelphia and the Conflict of Cliveden" presents the effects of the Battle of Germantown on Cliveden.

Lancaster, Bruce. *The American Revolution.* New York, NY: American Heritage Publishing Co., 1971. A comprehensive illustrated history of the American Revolution. Good drawings and illustrations.

Leiby, Adrian C. *The Revolutionary War in the Hackensack Valley.* New Brunswick, NJ: Rutgers University Press, 1962. Presents the History of Bergen County in the Revolution.

Lindemer, George C. *Teachers' Guide: Elementary* (New Jersey's Revolutionary Experience pamphlet #28). Trenton, NJ: New Jersey Historical Commission, 1975. Includes classroom activities, audio-visual materials, bibliography, and community resources.

Lundin, Leonard. *Cockpit of the Revolution: The War for Independence in New Jersey.* Princeton, NJ: Princeton University Press, 1940.

Martin, Joseph Plumb. *Private Yankee Doodle.* Philadelphia, PA: Acorn Press, 1979. Excellent first hand account of the Philadelphia Campaign and soldiers' life during the Revolution.

Morris, Richard. *Independence.* Washington, D.C.: U.S. Department of the Interior, 1982. A guidebook to Independence National Historical Park.

Morris, Robert. *The Truth About the Betsy Ross Story.* Beach Haven, NJ: Wynnehaven Publishing Co., 1982. Biography of Betsy Ross and history of the American Flag. Effectively refutes arguments claiming that Betsy Ross did not make the first flag.

Peterson, Harold L. *The Book of the Continental Soldier.* Harrisburg, PA: Stackpole Books, 1968. A well illustrated guide to the tools and equipment of the Continental Soldier.

Prince, Carl E. *Middlebrook — The American Eagle's Nest.* Somerville, NJ: Somerset Press, 1958. An in depth account of the Middlebrook Encampment.

Reed, John F. *Campaign to Valley Forge.* Union City, TN: Pioneer Press, n.d.

Reed, John F. *Valley Forge, Crucible of Victory.* Monmouth Beach, NJ: Philip Freneau Press, n.d.

Scheer, George F.,and Hugh F. Rankin, eds. *Rebels & Redcoats.* New York, NY: World Publishing Co., 1957. Eyewitness accounts of the Revolution.

Smith, Samuel S. *A Molly Pitcher Chronology.* Monmouth Beach, NJ: Phillip Freneau Press, 1972.

Smith, Samuel S. *Monmouth Battlefield in Maps and Pictures.* Monmouth Beach, NJ: Phillip Freneau Press, 1978.

Smith, Samuel S. *The Battle of Brandywine.* Monmouth Beach, NJ: Philip Freneau Press, 1976. Complete source on the Battle of Brandywine, includes illustrations of battle movements and list of American and British units that fought in the battle.

BIBLIOGRAPHY

Smith, Samuel S. *The Battle of Monmouth*. Trenton, NJ: New Jersey Historical Commission, 1978.

Smith, Samuel S. *The Battle of Princeton*. Monmouth Beach, NJ: Philip Freneau Press, 1967. Fine review of the military aspects of the Princeton Battle.

Smith, Samuel S. *The Battle of Trenton*. Monmouth Beach, NJ: Philip Freneau Press, 1965. Detailed account of the Battle of Trenton and the situation in New Jersey during December 1776.

Stryker, William S. *The Battle of Monmouth*. Princeton, NJ: Princeton University Press, 1927.

Stryker, William S. *The Battles of Trenton and Princeton*. New York, NY: n.p., 1898; Spartanburg, SC: The Reprint Company, 1967. Excellent overall account of the entire campaign of the "Ten Crucial Days."

Swan, Harry Kels, comp. *Raritan's Revolutionary Rebel: Frederick Frelinghuysen*. Somerville, NJ: Daughters of the American Revolution — Gen. Frelinghuysen Chapter, 1966.

Thayer, Theodore. *The Making of a Scapegoat: Washington and Lee at Monmouth*. New York, NY: Kennikat Press, 1976.

Thompson, Ray. *Washington at Germantown*. Fort Washington, PA: Bicentennial Press, 1971.

Tinkom, Harry M. and Margaret B.; Grant Miles Simon, F.A.I.A. *Historic Germantown*. Philadelphia, PA: American Philosophical Society, 1955. Explains the effects of the Battle of Germantown on the community.

Trevelyan, Sir George Otto, Bart. *The American Revolution*. 2nd ed. 2 vols. New York, NY: Longmans, Green & Co, 1899. A classic history of the Revolution, presents the British point of view.

Trussell, John B. B., Jr. *Birthplace of an Army*. Harrisburg, PA: Pennsylvania Historical & Museum Commission, 1983. Monograph on the Valley Forge encampment.

Trussell, John B. B., Jr. *The Battle of the Brandywine*, (Historic Pennsylvania Leaflet # 37). Harrisburg, PA: Pennsylvania Historical & Museum Commission, 1974. Good short summary of the Battle.

Trussell, John B. B., Jr. *The Battle of Germantown*, (Historic Pennsylvania Leaflet No. 38). Harrisburg, PA: Pennsylvania Historical & Museum Commission, 1974. Easy to read account of the military operations.

Ward, Christopher. *The War of the Revolution*. Ed. John R. Alden. 2 vols. New York, NY: The Macmillan Company, 1952. A good overview of the Revolution.

Weigley, Russell Frank. *Morristown, Morristown National Historical Park, New Jersey* (National Park Handbook #120). Washington, D.C.: U.S. Department of the Interior, 1983.

Widmer, Kemble. *The Christmas Campaign: The Ten Days of Trenton and Princeton*. Trenton, NJ: New Jersey Historical Commission, 1975. Fine, brief account of the "Ten Crucial Days."

BIBLIOGRAPHY

Wilbur, C. Keith. *Picture Book of the Continental Soldier.* Harrisburg, PA: Stackpole Books, 1969. Good source of information on the life of the Continental Soldier. Includes illustrations of tools, equipment, uniforms, and housing.

Wills, Garry. *Cincinnatus: George Washington and the Enlightenment.* Garden City, NY: Doubleday, 1984. This book presents images of George Washington through sculpture and painting, as well as his role as a leader throughtout his life.

Worton, Stanley N. *Teachers' Guide: Secondary* (New Jersey's Revolutionary Experience, Pamphlet #27). Trenton, NJ: New Jersey Historical Commission, 1975. Includes classroom activities, audio-visual materials, bibliography, and community resources.